China, After the Tour Bus Leaves

Diane -

Happy reading.

Ronald F. [illegible]

CHINA, AFTER THE TOUR BUS LEAVES

Ronald F. Dameron, Ph. D.

Foreword by

Dr. Franklin J. Woo

Dedication

This book is dedicated to my mother, Thelma Kingery. She is a farm woman, eighty-eight years young. She has raised eight children, and only she really knows how many grandchildren, great grandchildren, and now even great, great grandchildren she has.

Mom was our best correspondent in China. She wrote a letter every two weeks. She kept us informed of the happenings of the greater family, and she also included newspaper clippings of the major events at home.

When living in a foreign country one misses one's native food, particularly snack food. For Christmas Mom sent boxes of dried apricots, pears, and raisins. She even sent them airmail to be sure they arrived by Christmas. The air mail postage rate to China for three five pound boxes of dried fruit was over seventy-five dollars. To justify that expense, they would have to be pure gold. In China, for us, they were.

When we returned from China Mom had saved all of the letters that we had sent her. They were in a packet, sequentially numbered from one to thirty, and served as a useful reference in writing this book.

Thanks, Mom.
Ronald F. Dameron

Table of Contents

Acknowledgements

In today's society our young people are getting many opportunities for travel, and frequently their parents are expected to provide the home base. In this case Leona and I went off to China, and our three married children and their families provided the home base. When we returned from China they encouraged me to write a book, Dan even suggested the title, and they have all helped review the manuscript.

Thanks to Earl Arrants for developing all of my slide film while we were in China and for the photographic work in preparation for this book. Thanks to our many friends who wrote letters, sent Christmas cards, and special care packages. This support group helped us persevere.

I acknowledge the support from Ting Yen Ren and the Amity Foundation, Franklin Woo and the NCCC, and Bud Carroll and the General Board of Global Ministries and the United Methodist Church.

I also acknowledge the cooperation of *The Lodi News Sentinel* and *The Galt Herald* for printing my articles and for releasing them for use in this book.

I give special thanks to Foster Stockwell for his encouragement and for preparing the manuscript for printing.

Thank you one and all.

R. F. D.

Foreword

In April 1985 Christians and others in China created the Amity Foundation to seek assistance from churches and Christian organizations from abroad. The National Council of Churches of Christ in the U. S. A. was one of the first organizations to respond to the opening of China to the world.

Among the first group of teachers of English there were Leona Dameron and her husband Ron, who took early retirement from his position as superintendent of a school system in California. The two enthusiastic adventurers spent 1985-86 at the Nanjing Normal University as faculty members of the Foreign Languages Department. From there they made numerous forays to other (often remote) parts of China where they, especially Ron, shared their vast experiences as educators. After a brief interlude of four years in California, where they built their beautiful new home, the wandering Damerons decided in 1990 to spend another year teaching in China.

In this book readers can gain a profound sense of the rich experiences between Ron and Leona Dameron and the people of China. The pages are primarily about teaching English. By doing their assigned tasks well and with utmost integrity and professionalism, the Damerons made this activity into a medium where humanity touches humanity. They show that fundamentally teaching is the sharing of self. The Damerons are good representatives of the best in America. In China they shared generously their joys and aspirations, their concerns and exasperations and not least, their humor and their faith which sustained them. They are genuine bridge builders between China and the United States of America.

June 30, 1992

Franklin J. Woo—China Program Director, National Council of the Churches of Christ in the U.S.A.

Preface

China tours are popular with people around the world, but tourists in China are kept insulated and isolated from the Chinese people. The tours are billed as exotic and mysterious. "See the Great Wall, the Temple of Heaven, and the Forbidden City." Tourists follow a set itinerary. They stay in tourist hotels, travel in air conditioned buses to pre-determined sites, and eat banquet meals in private dining rooms separated from the Chinese guests. Only *After the Tour Bus Leaves* does one begin to get glimpses of everyday life in China.

My wife, Leona, and I went to China as part of a tour group in 1980. It was late June and the weather was delightful. In eighteen days we visited six cities, several factories and museums, and many ancient scenic spots. We had a glorious time. We stayed in four star hotels that were clean and comfortable. We bought souvenir silks, cloisonne vases, and sculptured hand woven carpets in the tourist Friendship Store, and through the window of an air conditioned tour bus we *saw China*.

In 1985/86 and again in 1990/91 Leona and I went back to China to teach English. One Sunday morning a tour group came into the Chinese Christian church. After the service we rushed over to greet them. We chatted enthusiastically for several minutes. "Where have you been?" "Where are you going next?" "What's the news at home?" Suddenly someone called to them. It was time to get back on the tour bus. They had an itinerary to keep. They seemed reluctant to leave. I watched the door close and the tour bus drive away. As I walked to where my bicycle was parked, I felt a sense of freedom. I had no schedule that day. I could go where I wanted. As I joined the Chinese bustle of bicycle traffic, I thought, I should write a book describing China *after the tour bus leaves.*

During one winter semester break we traveled to south China where we visited several cities. In Guilin we stayed in a tourist hotel. On the first floor there was a luxurious dining room with brocade drapes, white table cloths and artistically painted lacquer screens. We wanted to eat so I tried the door. It was secured with a large pad lock. I asked a passing hotel employee, "Why?"

He responded, "It is saved for the tour groups and this is not the tourist season." We were directed upstairs to a drab dining room on the third floor. This dining room had a bare cement floor. There were no cloths on the tables nor pictures on the walls. We ordered directly from the menu which was printed in Chinese. We had a bowl of soup, a bowl of rice, and a dish of cabbage with some little strings of twisted pork. This was life in China after the tour groups were gone.

While teaching in China we lived in university housing. When winter arrived, our apartment was cold; I mean it was in the low fifties for several months. I learned to type and to write on the black board with gloves on. Our Chinese students were also cold. In an attempt to keep warm in the unheated classroom we all wore many layers. We found that shared experiences, however, build relationships.

On another outing we were traveling to Gui Xi, a remote small city in south China where three of our students lived. It was late June and the heat and humidity reminded me of Charleston, South Carolina. We were playing *Running Fast*, a Chinese card game, with some of our Chinese friends, and kibitzers, total strangers, were leaning over our shoulders telling us which card to play. We were *seeing China* through the open train window—hard seat class does not have air conditioning—but we were also experiencing China all around us. I think that is the difference: after the tour is completed, after the tour bus leaves, that is when you start experiencing China, not just seeing it.

While we were living in China I wrote several articles for *The Lodi News Sentinel* and *The Galt Herald*, sharing observations and feelings as well as anecdotes and stories. I have included some of these articles in *China, After the Tour Bus Leaves*. To preserve the freshness of on-the-scene reporting, I have left many of them in the present tense.

China is a vast country. Seventy-eight percent of the people still live in the countryside. I do not present this book as a treatise on China, but as a way to share what I have observed and what I have experienced—*after the tour bus left.*

Ronald F. Dameron, Ph. D.
Retired teacher, principal, and public school superintendent

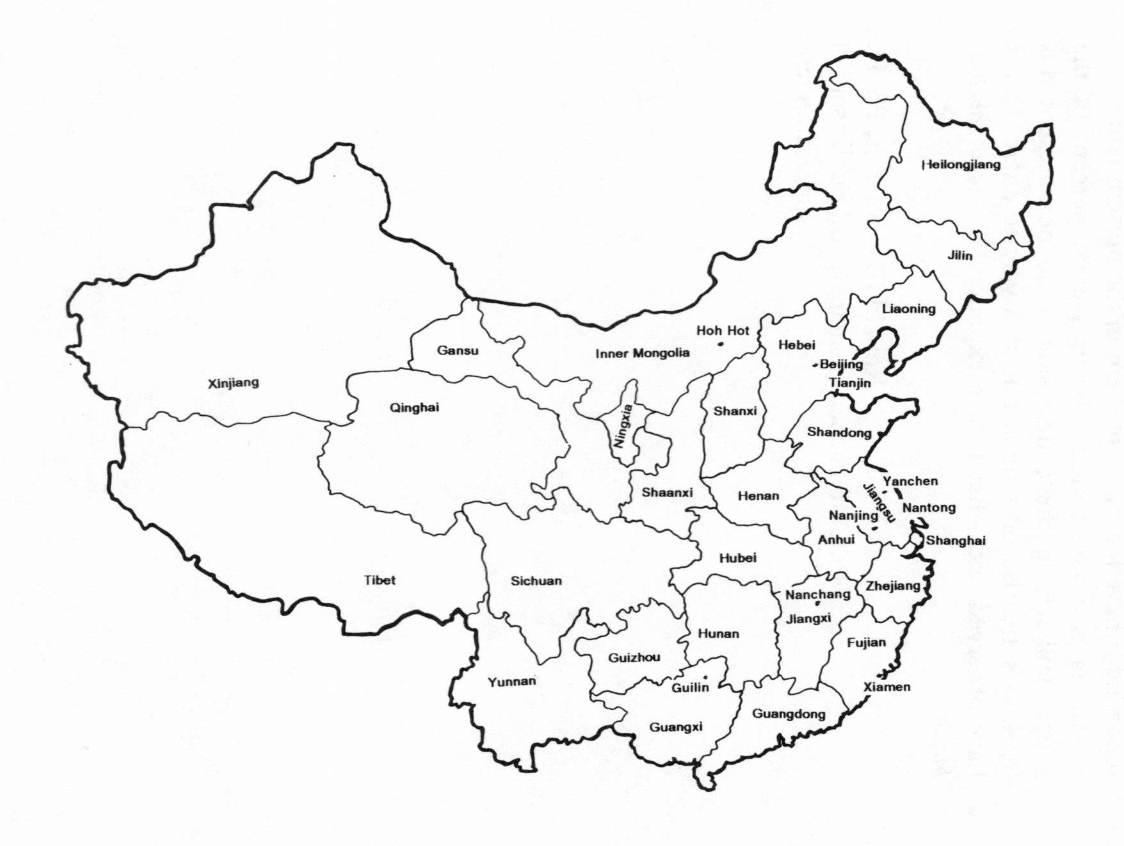
Heilongjiang
Jilin
Liaoning
Hoh Hot
Hebei
Beijing
Tianjin
Gansu
Inner Mongolia
Xinjiang
Qinghai
Ningxia
Shanxi
Shandong
Shaanxi
Henan
Yanchen
Jiangsu
Nantong
Nanjing
Anhui
Shanghai
Hubei
Tibet
Sichuan
Nanchang
Zhejiang
Jiangxi
Hunan
Fujian
Guizhou
Yunnan
Guilin
Xiamen
Guangdong
Guangxi

Chapter I

China Re-visited

It was a hot, muggy day towards the end of August. Although it was a daytime trip, we were traveling on a sleeper. I assume that was all that was available; the tour groups get the best trains. There were seventeen of us, Christian teachers of English, plus our Chinese hosts, and we were assigned eight to a compartment so four of us sat on a bed on each side. There had been a week of orientation in New York. We were on our way to Nanjing, a five hour train ride from Shanghai, where we would join with over seventy Christian teachers from all over the world for further orientation on Chinese language, customs, and teaching expectations. We would then be dispersed to six different provinces all over China.

It was crowded in our compartment—eight people plus all their carry-on luggage, and it was hot. We had a liter thermos of boiled water, but what we really needed was an ice chest. None of us had slept very well in the old classical style Shanghai hotel; we were too keyed up. By crossing the international date line we had lost a day and there were sixteen hours difference between Chinese time and the clocks in California. It was still yesterday morning in San Francisco. It would take several weeks for our systems to adjust to the time change, the humid climate, Chinese food, and the required boiled water.

My discomfort on the train, however, was more than off-set by the panorama of the Chinese countryside hurrying by outside my window. I could see fertile farm land divided into small rice, cotton, and vegetable fields- an occasional muddy, slow moving river, shallow ponds with flocks of ducks tended by old men or small boys. I saw picturesque boats in algae covered sloughs, some with long poles suspending fishing nets and some hauling bricks or sand or gravel. There were small villages with adobe brick houses and tile roofs, and two-hundred pound pigs were running free like pet dogs. There were small factories with towering smoke stacks billowing black and yellow smoke. The tall brick smoke stacks appear to be China's current pollution solution, waiting for human necessity to require better treatment.

The clackety clack of the train wheels going over the track joints, the swaying of the train car, the familiar scenery caused me to reflect back to 1985-86 when my wife, Leona, and I had first taught in China. We taught English at the Nanjing Teacher's University. We had been sponsored by the Amity Foundation, a non-governmental organization founded by a group of Chinese Christians in Nanjing in the spring of 1985. We had been in their first group of twenty-two Christian Teachers of English. I taught advanced English reading and writing to several classes of mostly English teachers and readings in western periodicals and newspapers to a class of sixty-four college juniors. My wife had taught English composition to first and second year students. Now, five years later, why had we come back?

I had retired from teaching and school administration back in 1985, and like a lot of retirees my wife and I wanted to travel, to see new country, to meet people, but now we had already done that. Also, living in China is not easy. We had minimal heat in our living quarters and no heat in the classrooms in Nanjing in 1985-86. The polluted air caused by millions of individual charcoal cooking fires and dust is hard on respiratory systems- my wife had had bronchitis for six weeks during the winter. Chinese food, boiled water, Asian toilets, government restrictions and censorship all take their toll. We also became homesick, particularly for our three married children and spouses, and five grandchildren- now six, so why did we return? Why were we here? Was this really a wise move?

Many people ask themselves the question, "What should one do after retirement?" Travel—then what? Play golf, or play bridge, or fish- that's what one does on one's day off, not on one's day on. We could watch television and go out to eat, but then we would have to sign up for an aerobics or other exercise program. No, we felt we needed to do something challenging to our talents and worthwhile for the community, whether local or world community. We have experience and training as teachers. With China's modernization there is a great need for teachers of English, and somehow, if we speak the same language, improved communication should increase the possibilities of working together in a peaceful world.

A major reason for returning to China had to be the friendships we had developed in China. We had continued to correspond with many of our students and colleagues from 1985/86, and as soon as we arrived at the hotel in Shanghai we had called Shen Bao. It was great to see him, his wife, and their son, now aged nine. I can remember when we first visited in their apartment. It was only one room. There was a double bed with Wang Bao's little bed next to it. The dining table was sandwiched between two portable cabinets. With only four feet of open floor space I was surprised to see a tricycle next to the bed. As we entered their apartment, Mrs. Bao left. Even though she spoke no English I was startled that she left. About twenty minutes later she returned with a package of ice cream which she promptly served. The Baos had no kitchen; they cooked out in the hall. While we were there the neighbor girl came in, and accidentally knocked over the night soil pot. The problem was aggravated by the lack of water to clean up the mess. To increase the water pressure for nearby construction their water was turned off during the daytime hours.

When we left their apartment that day, Wang Bao said, "*Zaijin, ye ye, ne ne,*" (Good bye, Grandpa and Grandma.)

We had a great visit. Shen Bao is no longer a teacher. He is the manager now of a tall hotel and office building in Shanghai. Mrs. Bao is a doctor and still rides the bicycle she bought from Leona five years before.

As exciting, and as worthwhile as our China trip might be, as I looked out that Chinese train window, I couldn't help but raise just a little doubt- why did we come back, and that question would pop up, unexpectedly at various times throughout the year. Just then an Amity colleague, on her first assignment, said, "Oh look at that huge water buffalo and at those Chinese workers carrying stuff with their bamboo poles. I'm sure glad I came."

"I am too," I said.

A Gift of Ginseng

When my wife and I had taught English in Nanjing in 1985-86 Leona had taught first and second year students, but I had taught mainly teachers and older community students. Since then many of these teachers and older students have scattered all over the world, doing postgraduate work in Canada, England, Australia, and the United States. We have continued to correspond with many of them. They write excellent English and their letters are a delight to read:

> During last semester I was studying and working at high pressure which almost made me a dull girl.

We had been considering returning to China to teach English at a university again, but the violent suppression of the student protests in Tiananmen Square in June of 1989 raised a cloud of uncertainty over the status of Chinese intellectuals and their relationship with foreigners. One of my students wrote:

> It is said that up to now the Chinese government still doesn't like common people, especially university students, to have too much contact with foreigners, mainly correspondents, and the topic of the Beijing incident is still a very sensitive one to be talked about.

When I notified Cherrie, one of my students now studying in Australia, that we were going back to China she was very excited and wrote me a lengthy letter. She described her studies, her part time job, and the Australian family she was staying with. She also made the following request:

> Would you be so kind to help me and my brother take some ginseng to China for our parents. This year is our parents 50 years golden anniversary and we want to give them ginseng as our presents.

She went on to say that Chinese believe ginseng is the best tonic for aged people.

I asked my wife, "What's ginseng?" Her sage reply was, "I don't know, but if it's legal, why don't they buy it in China?"

A few days later we visited a Chinese friend in Berkeley. "What's ginseng?" She said she did not know it by that name; what is it called in Chinese? We looked it up in her English/Chinese dictionary. It was not listed. Then she pulled out a larger dictionary.

"Oh, of course." "Yes, it is highly prized in China and considered very healthful, particularly for the elderly."

We asked her why they didn't buy it in China.

"Oh, it's very expensive."

For lunch we decided to go to Chinatown. Following lunch we walked in and out of the little shops, with their shelves efficiently saturated with Chinese merchandise designed to capture the eye of the tourist. Suddenly, almost jumping off the shelves to greet us, was a package of ginseng—4 ozs. The ginseng looked like dried roots that could have come from an Egyptian tomb. I asked the price of ginseng and the clerk said it varies according to the quality, but for one pound one hundred fifty dollars and up. In China that is equivalent to seven months salary for a classroom teacher.

I still had a lot of questions about taking ginseng into China. Cherrie's brother, Hua, was a student at Stanford, doing doctoral research on the properties of crystals for optics. We had visited him earlier in the year.

I called Mr. Hua. He was very excited. "I am so glad you are going to China and will take ginseng to our parents."

I was still skeptical. "Where in China do your parents live?"

"Wuxi!"

"Our train will be going through Wuxi, but we won't have time to stop and go look for your parents' house." His father is 83 and his mother 79.

"You are going to Nanjing?"

"Yes."

"No problem; I have two sisters in Nanjing. Just tell me your hotel and they will come and get it."

I persisted, "But how will you get the ginseng to me?"

Hua said, "Just tell me your flight number out of San Francisco and I will come to the airport."

I told him we did not have our flight number. We were going as part of a group of teachers and someone else was buying the tickets, but when we got them I would call him.

I was gone for a week, returned, and found Hua's message on the recorder and the tickets in the mail. I called

Hua. No one answered. I called that afternoon. No one answered. I called late that night- success.

"The flight number is 'One'. The time is 1:05, but being an international flight I want to be there two hours early, 11:00."

"No problem, I will be there at 10:00. I'll be there at 9:00."

"No, no." "Eleven o'clock will be fine."

* * *

At this point I do not know the rest of the story; our plane leaves San Francisco tomorrow. We have five large bags stuffed with clothes, food, teaching materials- including typewriter, tape recorder, slide projector, electric blanket and everything one needs to survive two years in an undeveloped province in China (Jiangxi Province), but I need to allow space for a pound of ginseng. Chinese customs regulations are strict, but they are also strange. They are particularly sensitive to printed materials, video tapes, medicines, foods--what about ginseng?

⋆ ⋆ ⋆

Our drive to the airport was uneventful; we made the trip in two hours. Hua was not there, but we were still early. About 10:45 Hua arrived with two 8 oz.

packages of ginseng, a small parcel securely wrapped in lined note book paper and an envelope with a name and phone number on it.

"What's this?"

"That's a letter to my father-in-law and his phone number in Nanjing and some perfume for him."

"Are you familiar with the Christian story of the birth of Christ?"

He said, "All I know is, this is 1990 and 1990 years ago he was born."

I said, "In the Bible it says that when Jesus was born, Wise Men came from the East bearing gifts of gold, frankincense and myrrh."

Hua asked, "What's frankincense and myrrh?"

I said, "It's something like ginseng and perfume."

The Chinese customs inspection still concerned me, but I had my letter of invitation from a Chinese university and I remained optimistic.

When we arrived in Shanghai I was the first one of our group to reach a customs counter. A young woman dressed in white officialdom looked at my passport, read my letter of welcome, and then started down my customs declaration form. I had not listed ginseng, but I had listed typewriter. At *typewriter* she stopped reading, said, "Just a minute," and went looking for higher authority. I waited. The rest of the group went to the various counters and began the process. I waited.

Finally the girl brought a young man dressed in blue officialdom. He looked at my papers, and then thumbed through two different books of customs regulations, and then said, "Just a minute," and left. The rest of the group completed their customs check and moved to a waiting room. Eventually the customs official returned, thumbed through his books again, and then wrote several things on my form. The girl prepared a brown envelope. The man put my papers in the envelope, sealed it, stamped it several times, and then gave it back to me saying, "Keep this." He did not look in any bag, and released me. The group clapped and cheered when I joined them. Chinese customs regulations are strange, but I still had the ginseng.

We arrived in Nanjing on Saturday afternoon. It was time to deliver my packages. I dialed the number on the envelope. "*Wei, wei.*" (Chinese for hello.) I asked if Wang Chi Gong were there. They did not understand the name. I switched to Chinese and explained I was an American from California and wanted to deliver a package to a Mr. Wang Chi Gong.

"What department is he in?"

I then realized I must have the telephone number of a university, but someone was there on a Saturday afternoon at 5:30. I said I did not know his department. The woman transferred me to the foreign affairs office. I again said, "I want to speak to a Mr. Wang Chi Gong." The Foreign Affairs Officer said, "Just a minute, I will ask my neighbors if anyone knows that name."

While I'm waiting all I can think of is, "I have carried this gift eleven thousand miles, and now I can't deliver it." Mr. Wang is Hua's father-in-law, but I didn't have any other information and the phone number is a university.

The Foreign Affairs Officer returned. "Is he the president of the university?"

I had to say, "I don't know," but things were falling into place. He was not in a department, and my Chinese friend would be too modest to tell me he was the president of the university. The operator rang the telephone extension of the president's home.

"Hello, when did you arrive?...I'll pick it up tomorrow." The perfume was for him, but he would see that the ginseng was delivered to Hua's father and mother in Wuxi.

Did I present the gifts to the president of the university the next day? No, he sent another son-in-law.

Guan Xi

Our teacher orientation was at the Ding Shan Hotel in Nanjing. *Shan* means mountain and the hotel was located on a hill with a nice view of the city. Our air conditioned rooms were comfortable and the food was good. We were now eating only with chop sticks, not the break-apart temporary wooden ones, but the smooth plastic durable kind. The beverages, tall bottles of Chinese beer, generic cola, and Chinese Seven-Up were all served at room temperature. Hot tea is served throughout the day, but never at mealtime.

One evening I got a call from the lobby. Someone had come to see me. I was very surprised. Who knew I was here? The young man, dressed in a long sleeved white shirt with the sleeves rolled once, looked familiar, but it took a minute for me to place him; he was one of my former students. He had been working full time, but had been enrolled in my evening class. I could not recall his name—Liu Lin Gui.

Mr. Liu greeted me warmly, said repeatedly how happy he was that I had returned to teach in China and inquired about our trip. I had enough experience in China to know these were all just preliminaries.

Then Mr. Liu said that he had just been accepted as a visiting scholar at San Diego State University, in California. My mind was racing ahead. He didn't need my help with the application; he was already accepted. He wouldn't be asking me to co-sign his financial support statement— not while I was living in China. What could he want?

Liu laid his heavy sheaf of papers on the table. He first showed me the application- yes, he had been accepted. He also had his financial statement. I was impressed. He had passed his TOEFL English fluency examination. As his English teacher that made me feel good. Finally, he showed me his application for a Visa. To me it looked routine, but to him, dealing with a governmental office, it seemed monumental.

Then the bombshell, the bottom line, the real reason why he wanted to see me.

"Do you know anyone in the American Consular Office in Shanghai?"

"No, I don't."

"Does anyone in your family know anyone in that office?"

"No."

"That is a pity, but would you write a letter, please, to the American Consulate Office that I can attach it to my visa application?"

I tried to explain to him that letters of influence were ineffective and inappropriate in governmental offices in the United States. He did not understand, nor believe me and continued to insist that I write a letter. I told him that he had his approval from San Diego State University. He had all the supporting documents that were required. He should have no problem with his visa application. He did not need a letter. I also reiterated that my letter to the consulate would be meaningless. I just could not see myself writing a letter- "Dear M— Consul, Mr. Liu is my friend; please give him a visa."

When we said our good byes, he was still disappointed that I wouldn't write a letter for him and was still quite sure that he would never get his visa without "knowing someone."

Guan Xi (pronounced gwan she) is prevalent in all aspects of Chinese society. *Guan Xi* means "paving the way," "bypassing lines," or "opening doors" that otherwise would remain closed. During our two years in China we experienced *guan xi* in many forms.

We had accumulated many pieces of porcelain. Jingdezhen, the historic Chinese city where the process of porcelain making was developed over a thousand years ago, was only five hours away by bus or train. We had purchased some of the porcelain, but other pieces came as gifts- hand painted decorative plates, beautiful egg shell porcelain vases, panda bears, tri-color horses in various poses and even a lady Buddha that brought you good luck as she dripped water from a pitcher into the mouth of a dragon. After a year in China our luggage had grown beyond allowable limits. We had a dilemma.

"Hey, what are we going to do with all this porcelain?"

"Well, some of it is beautiful and I want to take it home."

"But you can't carry it all. It's too heavy. And some of the prettiest is *eggshell* porcelain and very fragile."

"Do you think we could ship part of it; you know, have a wooden box made, and wrap each piece separately. Maybe we could use some of that styrofoam for packing material."

"Let's try it. Even if one or two items get broken, we'll get most of them home."

We carefully wrapped each piece in half inch styrofoam sheeting, placed everything in a cardboard box, and then, in conformity with Chinese postal regulations, placed the cardboard box inside a thin plywood wooden box that the carpenter's shop had made for us.

We did not seal the boxes because Chinese postal authorities must examine the contents of packages before they are mailed. We stuffed our pockets with tape for the cardboard box and hammer and nails for the wooden box, tied everything on our bicycles and headed for the post office. I normally went by myself, but anticipating a more complex operation, I asked the administrative assistant from our university Training Center to go with me and serve as interpreter.

At the downtown post office the clerk sifted through the box, unwrapped several pieces and after examining them, promptly declared that she would not accept it.

"Everything will break!"

I had the interpreter explain that each piece was wrapped in protective material and everything was in a wooden box as required.

The clerk said, "Wait and talk with my supervisor."

My interpreter then told me, "You wait here. I know one of the employees up on the fourth floor. I will go and get him."

A few minutes later my interpreter returned with a young man in a white postal uniform, about the same time the supervisor arrived. The supervisor told me in English, "You may not mail this because everything will be broken." Then she added, "Oh, it won't be broken in China, only after it arrives in America."

I insisted that I wanted to mail it. The young postal employee, the friend of my interpreter, did not say anything. At no time did he make any attempt to enter into the conversation. He was simply there.

The supervisor asked me, "How much do you think it will weigh?" I estimated eleven kilos. (A kilo is 2.2 pounds.)

She said, "That will cost you about 300 yuan, and everything will be broken. Do you still want to mail it?"

I asked, "What good is all this stuff to me if I cannot send it home?"

She said, "If you do not mail it, at least you won't be out the 300 yuan." (She had a legitimate point since 300 yuan is equivalent to about three month's salary for a middle school teacher.) Our "*guan xi* friend" said nothing.

I said that I still wanted to mail it. She made me sign a form releasing the post office from all responsibility for breakage. She weighed the box and even though it weighed only a fraction over eleven kilos, she charged me 430 yuan and 80 fen. I was shocked at the amount.

Our postal employee friend returned to his fourth floor work area without ever having said a word, but his presence had fulfilled his obligation to his friend. (For the reader's information- only one of the dozen or so pieces of porcelain broke during the three and a half month mail trip to California.)

Guan xi can be displayed in little ways. My interpreter accompanied me to the health clinic. There was a line. About a dozen people were waiting at the window. He went around the line and talked to someone through a side window. I was able to go in immediately.

Some form of *guan xi* is frequently required to purchase train tickets. My wife and I took an overnight train from Beijing to Inner Mongolia. Our student in Beijing went to the train station at 5:00 in the morning to make sure he would be able to buy our tickets. He had no trouble. It took him five minutes. In China, however, you cannot buy round-trip tickets, so after spending several days in Inner Mongolia, we needed tickets to return.

Our friend in Inner Mongolia, Shang Zhi Cong, went to the ticket office on Monday afternoon. They told him the tickets for Wednesday night were not available yet- come back tomorrow. Shang then went to the ticket office Tuesday morning at five o'clock. As he entered the room he was given a number—#55. When he went to the ticket window they said there were only sixteen sleeping berths available and they were all sold out. Shang observed that others in the room had already had priority numbers when they walked in the door.

I told Shang we had to have tickets for Wednesday night so that afternoon he and I went to the office of the station master. When we entered his office he was on the telephone. I went up to his desk and laid my business card in Chinese on the desk. When he hung up, he read my card and then pulled out his cards and gave me one. I greeted him, shook his hand, and said we needed tickets for the next night back to Beijing. I then presented him my letter of introduction from my university. He was very gracious. He took my letter, and with a flourish wrote a personal endorsement on it, and said, "Pick up your tickets tomorrow morning."

We thanked him and left. Shang went to the ticket office the next morning, showed them the letter with the station master's endorsement, and without incident, bought two tickets, for two of the sixteen berths which had been **sold out** the previous day.

Joanne was an attractive middle school teacher, aged twenty-eight, and still single. She was tall and had an engaging smile. She was almost married at one time, having actually lived with a man for a brief period of time, but the marriage never took place and now she was free and independent again. But somehow, her current principal found out about her past relationship and considered her behavior immoral by Chinese standards. The principal has removed her from her regular teaching position and only used her as an occasional substitute.

Joanne was quite distraught. She liked to teach. She waned to teach, but she felt there was nothing she could do to improve the situation. I asked Joanne if she could get a job somewhere else. She told us, "Teaching is considered an essential profession and I would need an official release from teaching by the government to take a job as a secretary or some other non-teaching job." I asked what she needed to do then to get re-instated, slip the principal some money? Joanne said that many of the other teachers gave the principal money, especially at holiday time. I asked, "How much?" Joanne said, "I don't know. They would give him perhaps, a package of cigarettes and each cigarette would be wrapped in a bill." Joanne said she really did not want to do that.

Anyone can buy a refrigerator, but if you want to buy a higher quality one made in Japan, you have to know someone.

Currently the postage for an airmail letter from China to the United States is two yuan, and it is difficult to buy any two yuan stamps other than the common one with the picture of a Chinese Buddha. If you go to the park, however, you can buy anything you want from the free-market stamp vendors at an increased price. They not only sell historic and canceled stamps, they have sheet after sheet of the current stamps that are not available at the post office.

One day a middle-aged gregarious postal clerk asked me if I would exchange some Chinese Foreign Exchange Currency for her *Ren min bi*, or people's money. It is difficult for the average person to get foreign exchange currency and on the black market the exchange rate was about 1.4:1. I told her, "Later."

About ten days later I went to her post office counter and gave her fifty yuan in foreign exchange currency. She reached for a small bag pinned just inside her skirt and came up with fifty yuan in *ren min bi*. Two weeks later I gave her a hundred more, again for an even exchange.

From then on she saved every new stamp that was issued and provided me with enough duplicates for my friends. She sold them to me at face value. Our friendship never extended beyond the post office, but whenever I was in the neighborhood I would stop at her window just to say, "Hi."

In a country where people do not have a lot of money, it is nice to have friends.

Time *Trial*

On the Friday before classes began in Nanjing Teachers University in 1985, the phone rang in our apartment. I was in the department office checking on my classes. Leona took the call. When I returned she told me the following. A Mr. Garrelli (not his real name) had called from Beijing. He had identified himself as the Beijing news correspondent for *Time* magazine. He said he was writing a story on the newly formed Amity Foundation, and he wanted to include some pictures. Since Leona and I were part of that first group of Amity teachers, he asked, "Do you have any colored slides of you and your husband teaching Chinese students?" Leona had told him that our classes would not begin until Monday, but that we did have slide film and that we could take pictures in our classrooms on Monday. Mr. Garrelli said he would "Call us back on Monday evening with further instructions."

I told Leona this sounded like a spy thriller—we did not know this Mr. Garrelli; he was purportedly a correspondent from Beijing, and he would call us back with further instructions. Our egos soon took command, however, the excitement of appearing in a world wide magazine was motivation enough to proceed.

On Monday morning, armed with our new camera and a roll of high speed Kodachrome film, Leona and I went to the department office. Leona was greeted with the news, "You will not meet with your freshmen classes for two weeks. They have gone on their military training." Before entering a Chinese university students attend a military training camp and receive training in discipline, military drill, basic fire arms, and political studies. Some of the other classes would meet later in the week. None of our classes would meet today. What to do?

We found an empty classroom. We found several students, but none of them were our students. We could not wait. Mr. Garrelli would call back tonight.

"Would you like to be in *Time* magazine?" "May we take your picture?" Everyone was excited about the prospects of their picture being in a western magazine, so they were quite willing and enthusiastically cooperated as we created simulated student-teacher interactions. I took pictures of Leona helping students and then she took pictures of me. We stood at the lectern, we leaned over students at their desks, we pointed at maps on the wall. The pictures, though simulated, portrayed real students: the young women were all short, had black hair, and all of them were very slender. Dressed primarily in skirts and blouses, they were well groomed and attractive.

The young men were also short and slender. Their dress was not attractive- white shirts with short sleeves or long sleeves partly rolled and baggy pants. They were polite and responsive to our requests. We completed one full roll of film and were quite satisfied with the results. Now we would wait for the phone call "for further instructions."

That evening, in our apartment, we waited nervously for Mr. Garrelli's call. We were nervous because we did not know what to expect. When the call came, Leona answered it.

"Hello, is this Mrs. Dameron?"

"Yes, it is."

"How are things going with you and your husband in Nanjing?"

"Everything is fine."

"Have you been able to take pictures of your teaching for me?"

"Yes, but what are we supposed to do with the film?"

"Unfortunately, I will not be able to come to Nanjing to pick up the film, but I will need the film tomorrow. Can you fly the film to me?"

"How?"

"Take it to the Nanjing airport and give it to any American businessman who is flying to Beijing. There is a flight tomorrow evening. I will wait for the film in the Beijing airport. I will be holding a sign *Time* magazine."

"Good grief." "Is he aware this is China?" "How will we get to the airport?" We could not jump in our car and drive to the airport as we would in the United States. It was too far to ride our bicycles, and we had no idea what the bus schedule was. We decided to go to the Foreign Affairs Office of the university and request a car.

"We will provide a car and a driver, but we must charge you for the use of the car."

"Why must we pay for the car?"

"Because it is for your personal use."

"We wish to go to the airport in order to deliver a roll of film portraying our teaching students from *Nanshida* (Chinese for Nanjing Teachers University). Think of the importance to your university to have these pictures in *Time* Magazine."

He agreed to let us use the car without fee.

That evening Leona and I and an interpreter went to the Nanjing airport. We felt very uncomfortable. Nanjing is a city of over three million people, but the airport is tiny. What if there are no American businessmen flying to Beijing tonight? What if Chinese authorities start asking questions? We had only been in China two weeks and we didn't want our stay to come to a quick termination.

When we walked into the waiting room, all I could see were Chinese people. Then we walked into another waiting room. There we saw two men with brown hair, dressed in western sport coats, but their most distinguished feature, they were a full head taller than anyone around them. They were carrying new cases of some kind of equipment.

I went up to them and asked if they were Americans.

One of them said, "We're from Texas."

I told them we were teachers in a local university.

The other one said, "They sure roll up the sidewalks at sundown in this city." The remark reminded me that western businessmen in China lead a different lifestyle than we teachers did. I learned that they were both from the 3M company in Austin. I also learned that they had a sense of humor.

"I have this roll of film and I wonder if you would be willing to carry it to Beijing for me?"

"What are the pictures of—airports and bridges?"

"Sh, sh!" "Do you want to get us all in trouble?" I quickly looked around, but no one seemed to be listening.

I explained the situation, and they were happy to take the film. We went back to the university and hoped Mr. Garrelli would be at the other end of the flight.

When one first arrives in China he/she writes many letters. In the next *umpteen* letters home we told everybody, "Check the *Time* magazine; look for our pictures." The article was never published, but about a month later I received a package in the mail. It was sixty-five *Time* magazines for my Readings in Western Periodicals and Newspapers class.

Chapter II

What a Life

Foreign teachers are provided housing on the university or college campuses where they teach. At Jiangxi Normal University we lived in the Foreign Guest House along with five other foreign teachers. Leona and I are from California, and the five other foreigners were all from Colorado. It did not matter where we were from; to the Chinese we were always "foreigners." We were called "foreign guests," or "foreign teachers," or "foreign experts," but always "foreigners."

Leona and I were given a living room/study, a bedroom and a bathroom. A thin carpet covered the cement floor. There was no pad under the carpet and the carpet did not quite reach the walls. We were unimpressed until our students came to visit. When they entered the room and saw the carpet, they immediately asked if they should take off their shoes. The walls were cement which made it very difficult to hang up pictures. Chinese homes do not display the voluminous pictures and wall hangings that American homes display.

We had a small Chinese refrigerator, two study desks with lamps, two uncomfortable stuffed chairs, a firm but comfortable bed, and feather pillows that seemed to have more than feathers in them—maybe the chicken's wings and feet? We soon traded them for pillows with rice hulls.

Our bathroom was large, had a tile floor, and was brightened by five large windows. We felt very blessed until the winter season arrived. Then the windows proved to be very cold. Unfortunately the toilet always leaked, sometimes internally and sometimes out across the floor to the floor drain. Plumbing does not have a very high priority in China. The shower constantly dripped into a badly stained bath tub. Sometimes we had hot water, but whenever we showered there were no shower curtains and the water sprayed out onto the floor and sort of drained to the floor drain.

We had a new little washing machine with a separate tub for spin dry which was a great advantage in a climate with high humidity. The hot water would generally arrive in time for the second rinse, so as soon as we finished the laundry we could take a hot shower.

We were also provided with maid service. Each day our maid, a Chinese woman in her late fifties, brought three liter-sized thermoses of boiled water, emptied the waste paper basket, cleaned the bath room, and swept the carpet with a whisk broom. A couple months after we arrived we discovered there was a vacuum cleaner in the house. It was a tank type vacuum cleaner made in China. From then on the maid used the vacuum in our room about once a month.

Although our living quarters were rather austere, by American standards, we knew we were in China and adjusted to the conditions rather easily. Our greatest discomfort, however, was the cold. In South China (south of the Yangtze River) there is no heat in any of the homes or apartments. School children wear many layers of clothing when they go to their unheated classrooms. University dormitories have cement floors and cement walls which accentuate the cold. Offices and stores and banks and churches are cold as well. There is no place to go to ever get warm.

Foreigners are given special treatment. We had a heat pump in our bedroom window. Unfortunately, heat pumps without supplementary heat strips, become less efficient as the temperature drops. Our heat pump worked great in October when we didn't need it, but during the five months of winter it was generally ineffective. Throughout the winter months the temperature in our living room/study was in the high forties or low fifties. We put on long underwear in December, added a second layer of long underwear in January, and continued to wear at least one layer until the first of May. By May 9th we were in short sleeves. Our Middle School Teachers Supervisory Committee met in our apartment. During the informal banter before every meeting, our Chinese colleagues would always ask, "Are you dressed warm enough; are you wearing enough clothes?" We would promptly pull up a pants leg or fold down our collar to show how many layers we were wearing. Their persistent response was always, "That is not enough; wear more clothes."

It snowed two inches the first week in January and our inside temperature dropped to forty-three degrees. The heat pump raised that temperature only five degrees. I bought sheets of half inch foam and covered the windows every night. We had an electric blanket and went to bed early. In spite of this my fingers and toes began to swell and I got brown splotches—chill blains. Our medical book said this was not caused by severe cold, but by prolonged cold. It reached the point where Leona and I would sit at our desks, trying to type or read, and keep looking at our watch and asking each other, "Is it time to go to bed yet; is it time to go to bed yet?"

One day we rode our bicycles to the tourist hotel. We wanted to buy some chocolate bars. About ten minutes after we entered the hotel, we looked at each other and said, "Let's go." We were wearing so many clothes, we couldn't stay in a heated room. There is a limit to how many layers one can take off in public.

One of our Chinese students knitted a pair of gloves without finger tips for me. I used them as my "inside" gloves and wore them constantly—I could write with them; I could type with them. I could even wear them while eating with chop sticks. (I wore regular gloves for outside activities, including when I rode my bicycle.)

Our Foreign Guest House had a lovely court yard, a protective perimeter wall, a gate house where visitors including our students were required to register, and additional rooms where Chinese dignitaries and overseas Chinese tourists could stay for a short term. A comfortable reception room with colored television was available, but since all the programs were in Chinese, the foreign guests seldom used it.

There were two small drab dining rooms, one for the foreigners and one for the Chinese. Overseas Chinese are not considered to be foreigners. A Chinese cook, a sixty year old man, prepared three meals per day, six days a week. It was our idea to give him Sundays off.

Breakfast consisted of rice gruel, two bread rolls, an egg, and a glass of hot powdered milk. There are few dairy cows in China, but through a United Nations program, powdered milk is available. Occasionally this menu changed to *you tiao,* (fried dough), or steamed bread with rice gruel. *You tiao* are made from dough that is deep fried like a doughnut, but without the sugar, and rice gruel is just watery rice. We had rice gruel every morning for breakfast the entire year. The students were also served rice gruel in the student dining room, although their rice gruel was considerably more watery. Sometimes in restaurants they do not even provide a spoon for rice gruel. It is so thin one is expected to tip up the bowl and drink it.

Lunch and dinner was rice, soup, and two dishes. One dish would be a vegetable, such as eggplant, cucumbers, winter melon, cabbage, squash, garlic shoots, or string beans. The other dish would be a vegetable with little strings of pork or perhaps scrambled eggs with stewed tomatoes. Chicken and fish were seldom served; they were considered too expensive even though we paid for our meals. There was no beef, even in the markets. Since exotic food is expensive, our meals remained very basic.

The dining room was unheated and we placed a brick against the door to block the wind blowing through the hall. In February the house manager bought an electric portable heater for our dining room, and after that we seven Americans lingered at the dining table long after we finished eating, much to the dismay of the Chinese girl who washed the dishes.

Shopping in China[1]

When you first arrive in China, there are many things you need to buy just to get settled. Many of us feel we were *born to shop*, but buying things in China is different—sometimes fun, sometimes frustrating, but always an *experience*.

It was Sunday. The streets were jammed with people, bicycles, pull carts and noise. The street was under construction and the buses were not running. We had been confined to walking distance of the university ever since we arrived—three days—and we had to have wheels. We walked the two miles to the Friendship Store and at the entrance were swept inside by the crowds. In Nanjing in 1985/86 the Friendship Store was reserved for foreigners and overseas Chinese, but tourists never went to Nanchang, so this Friendship Store was open for everyone. The store aisles were solid humanity. Western people are accustomed to space; if we do not have space around our person, we feel very uncomfortable. In China there is no space; there are too many people. Walking through the crowds, I felt like the ball in a pin ball machine. I bumped into someone, turned to say excuse me, and the person never even looked back. In the pockets and eddies of the stream of people,

---

[1] Written for *The Lodi News Sentinel* while I was still in China and published on Nov. 17, 1990.

however, we were constantly approached by black market requests, "change-a-money." We resisted the temptation even though the mark-up is something like forty percent.

We found lots of Forever women's bicycles, a top quality brand made in Shanghai, but there were three listed prices. One price was in *ren min bi* or people's money, a lower price in the foreign exchange certificates and a price even lower that was designated *special.* We agreed to buy one of the bicycles and requested the special price. They refused to give us the special price, and we never found out who the special price was for. The foreign exchange certificate price was 259.20 including a lock (that is equivalent to about fifty-five dollars in United States currency.) Leona handed the clerk three one-hundred yuan bills, and he proceeded to write up the receipt for three hundred yuan. Leona strongly objected: they talked for several minutes, he in Chinese and Leona in Chinglish and finally they agreed on the price of two-hundred sixty yuan. We realized later that he did not have any change and was therefore rounding it off, rather generously.

It was more difficult finding a man's bicycle for some reason. Their first response was *mei you* (don't have.) But we kept looking and finally found one in a group of damaged bicycles that had been marked down. In addition to a dent in the cross bar, the seat was broken. I asked the clerk to switch the broken seat with one from another damaged bicycle and bought it for 238.80 yuan, rounded up to 240 yuan. Now, store aisles that had been so crowded we had trouble walking in, became an even greater challenge to wheel our new bicycles out.

Bicycle locks are required in China. Since my bicycle had been damaged, I had to buy the lock separately and now had to get it installed. Fortunately, with so many bicycles in China there is a sidewalk bicycle repairman almost every other block. The repairman we selected had no *overhead*, literally. He had a small box of parts, a tire patching kit, and a tire pump. He worked by himself except for four loungers. The man was efficient, and courteous, and charged us more than he would have charged a local, but we didn't mind the price—three yuan (equivalent to about sixty cents in United States currency.) I gave the man three yuan, two in local money—that was all I had—and one in foreign exchange currency. The repairman passed the tourist money (the foreign exchange currency yuan) to the four friends so that they could see what one looked like. We felt we got our money's worth in the picture Leona was able to take while the loungers were all looking at the **funny money**.

On another occasion I went to the department store and asked a clerk, partly in Chinese, partly with hand gestures, where I could buy a paring knife. Paring knives are essential because in China one does not eat apples without peeling them. She pointed to the other side of the store. I walked in the direction she pointed and wandered around for several minutes looking for the right counter. A young woman carrying a baby walked up and motioned for me to follow her. She was not a store employee. I followed her clear out to the entrance of the store and there she pointed to a counter, filled with paring knives. Without saying a word, she nodded her head and left.

Eastern China is so humid during the summer that sugar gets hard as a brick if you leave it sitting around, so I only wanted one *jin*, (about a pound.) The clerk put a plastic bag with two *jin* of sugar on the counter. I requested only one *jin*. She took another bag and placed it on the scales. Then with a metal scooper she gradually filled it with one *jin* of sugar. But in the process she tore a hole in the original bag with the metal scooper and gradually spilled about a cupful out on the counter. After my bag was measured and secured, she took her hand and wiped the spilled sugar from the counter into another container to have it ready for the next customer. To appreciate the real impact for me, you have to appreciate how dirty everything is in China, including store counters.

When you have bicycles it is fun just to ride around and explore new areas.

"Let's turn here; doesn't this road lead to the park?"

We were not prepared for what we saw. The street was little more than an alley. There were so many people, and bicycles, and carts we had trouble getting through, even on bicycles. Free market vendors displayed their wares—merchandise of every description. First there were carts filled with apples, oranges and bananas. Then came the meat, raw pork laying exposed on wooden tables, and young men with meat cleavers waiting to serve you. Point to what you want; they will cut it off and hand it to you. Bring your own container. The vegetables came next, displayed in baskets or laying in piles on canvas or plastic on the sidewalk. There were onions and garlic, cabbage and cauliflower, string beans and cucumbers, and winter melon.

Our first reaction was to the sight—the mass, the motion, the activity. Then we heard the sounds—of the crowd, and the ringing of bicycle bells. Then we became aware of the smell—a combination of garlic and overflowing garbage containers, of ducks and chickens with their feet tied, and *jiaozis* (dumplings) and oil sticks cooking over charcoal fires.

Beyond the produce was plastic ware, inflatable toys, helium filled balloons and bicycle baskets.

"Yes, let's stop."

We were away from the university and off the main streets so we attracted a small crowd instantly. The young man talked to us in the local dialect and we could not understand him and he could not understand us so he immediately gave up, took several steps back to where his bowl of noodles was and resumed eating. We were persistent because he had baskets we might want. He returned and showed us incorrectly how the brace attached and showed us only one of the two brackets we knew we needed. He retreated. A lady got into the act. Chinese bystanders will help you whether you need it or not. By the time they get through you usually do. When we finally got to the question "How much?" and we couldn't understand the local dialect for yuan, the poor vendor almost gave up again, but with superfluous help from the bystander and our estimate of about how much it should be, we negotiated a price, seven-fifty, gave him a ten yuan note, and received a fistful of paper change in return. I shoved it into my pocket without counting it and we went home. Back in our apartment Leona asked, "How much change did you get?" I threw the pile of wadded up paper on the bed and counted it: I had the correct change, two yuan, fifty fen, and the basket is just what we wanted. ("Fools go in where . . .")

We have purchased paper clips, just a bit rusty, but they work fine, and rubber bands that they sell for one fen each; we bought ten. I went to a large vegetable market looking for potatoes. I finally found some—in an old man's basket. I asked in Chinese where he found them, and he pointed to the proper area. We have purchased apples and bananas and plastic sandals. We have also bought a screw driver, pliers, and a crescent wrench. There are little stories connected with each of these. We can also buy Pepsi Cola and Sprite. The labels are in Chinese characters, but we can tell what they are by the colored logo on the label.

I wanted to mail two letters. Chinese envelopes and Chinese stamps have no glue. Every post office has a paste pot, but seldom a brush to apply the paste, so most people use their fingers. Our post office has a towel and a wash pan of water to wash the paste off your fingers. Hundreds of people come into that post office every day and they all wipe their fingers on that one towel. The towel and wash pan reminded me of stories in the Old West where they hung a towel by the wash tub outside the Inn where their guests were expected to wash their hands and people wondered if the towel were actually clean that morning when the first person used it. To avoid the paste pot and the towel and wash basin, I wanted to buy some extra stamps. I could then glue them on at home with my own glue stick. I placed two letters on the counter and in Chinese requested four stamps. Frequently in China when foreigners speak Chinese, the Chinese doubt the foreigner's statement because they obviously know what the foreigner really wants. The clerk gave me two stamps. I requested four. She pointed to my two letters and said that was all I needed. I repeated my request for four stamps. She continued to argue. I put both stamps in my wallet, pushed my letters forward and said, "Now I only need two more." She gave me the other two stamps. Then she calculated my change incorrectly. I retrieved the stamps from my wallet, laid them back on the counter, and added up the bill. Only then did she give me the proper change. When I stepped away from the counter a girl said in perfect English, "Your Chinese is very good." (My Chinese is very limited, but I appreciated the compliment.) It turned out she was a senior in the local middle school and her English was very good. (How many of us know Chinese?) Yes, for communication in the world I place my hopes on their learning English. That, after all, is why we went to China.

Frustration[2]

I did not intend to write this story. Actually things have been going rather well, but sometimes life's greatest frustrations are those things that hit us unexpectedly.

China has two kinds of currency, *ren min bi* for Chinese citizens and *foreign exchange certificates* for tourists. As teachers in China we are given a residence card so that we may spend either kind of currency. In fact, our salaries are paid partly in local money and partly in foreign exchange certificates.

The foreign currency portion of our salary is paid directly by our sponsoring agency in Nanjing. We were requested to open a receiving account in the local Bank of China so the money could be deposited by mail.

We went to our department and said we needed to go to the bank.

They said, "It is very far."

---

[2] Published in *The Lodi News Sentinel* on Nov. 17, 1990.

We said, "We can go by bus."

"No, the street is torn up now and the bus cannot go through until the street is repaired. Perhaps we can get a car."

We waited. They returned and said, "There is no car." "All of the vehicles have gone to the central square where there is a celebration now for the *holy fire* (The Asian Games version of the Olympic Torch). We will order a car for Monday."

On Monday morning at 8:00 Leona and I were taken in an elderly van to the Bank of China. We arrived at 8:30. The doors were open so we walked into the lobby. We asked an employee where we should go to open an account. "I'm sorry, that department does not open until 9:00."

We said, "O.K., we will just go in and sit down and wait until 9:00."

On Sunday morning Leona and I walked two miles to the Friendship Store to purchase bicycles. On Sundays the schools and many of the factories and businesses are closed so it is a big shopping day in China. The Friendship Store was a mad house. In the crowds of shoppers we were approached at least six times by young men asking to "change-a-money." Foreign exchange certificates are essential for foreign imports such as Coca cola, Kodak film, and specialized foods, international travel, and applications for studying abroad, and yet it is very difficult for local Chinese to acquire it. We did not want to participate in the black market even though we were desperate for some ren min bi. We needed to do a lot of local shopping, and we would not receive our first month's *ren min bi* salary for two more weeks. So we rejected each request to change money, telling ourselves, "We are going to the bank tomorrow. We can change it then."

He said, "No, I'm sorry, there is a meeting and you cannot go in and sit down."

"O.K., we will wait in the van."

At 9:00 we were taken to the counter which said, "Foreign Deposits." Leona said she would like to open an account in United States dollars and handed them a twenty dollar bill.

"I'm sorry, but for twenty dollars, there is an exchange fee. Your account balance will be $19.40."

"Excuse me, we do not want to exchange any money. This is United States dollars. We want to open an account for U. S. dollars and deposit this twenty dollar bill."

"You may open an account in U. S. dollars. Your beginning balance will be $19.40."

We assumed the bank was charging an up front fee for establishing an account so we went ahead with the transaction, opening the account in Leona's name. Then I presented the same clerk with a one hundred yuan note and said that I would like to open an account in foreign exchange certificates.

"I'm sorry, but you can only have an account in U. S. dollars."

"But I will be paid in foreign exchange certificates. My salary will be sent to this bank in foreign exchange certificates for deposit. Later I will withdraw the money in foreign exchange certificates because I can only spend it as F. E. C. I want an account in foreign exchange certificates." My disbelief was reinforced by the fact that four years ago I had an account in Nanjing in foreign exchange certificates.

The clerk said, "Sorry."

"I would like to talk with someone else please."

My interpreter said, "There is no one else to talk to."

"There are a hundred employees in this bank. I want a second opinion."

Our interpreter said, "She is the only one who can open an account for you."

While we were at the bank we wanted to make sure we got some foreign exchange certificates changed into *ren min bi*. We went to the counter that was labelled "money changing." There were three clerks sitting at their desks plus one empty chair. I presented a one hundred yuan F. E. C. note and requested it be changed into *ren min bi*.

"I'm sorry, the person who does that is not here right now. Please come back at ten o'clock."

What's Thanksgiving Without Pie?

"If I'm going to bake a pie, I will need some flour."

"O. K., there has to be some flour out there somewhere."

We first tried the store directly across the street from the university. "*Ni you mei you mian fen?*" (Do you have any flour?)

"*Mei you.*" (No.)

We didn't really think they would have any, so the important question was, "*Zai nar*?" (Where can we get some?) The clerk pointed in the direction of the alley where all the free market vendors are. We walked down the alley and then asked at a shop that looked promising. The clerk said they did not have any flour and in response to the question, "Where can we get some?" she pointed vaguely on down the alley. We walked another hundred feet and asked at another shop. The same vague hand motion was given, pointing on down the alley. After repeating this procedure several times we arrived at the corner where I had previously purchased cooking oil. The store sold various grains in bulk and packaged noodles. I was optimistic. I went up to the counter and asked if I could buy some flour. "*Mei you.*" I asked where I could get flour. The clerk repeated, "*Mei you.*" This expression is overused in China. It not only means that I do not have any, it can also mean that I am not interested in helping you any further. I persisted with the Chinese question, "Where?" and finally a young man in his twenties stepped up and asked, "May I help you?" I said I wanted to know where I could buy some flour. By this time five or six customers had gathered in curiosity, just to watch these foreigners. My Chinese benefactor turned to the crowd and they all talked in Chinese like they were deciding on who to run for congress. Then the young man turned to us and said, "Follow me."

Leona and I went outside the store, and when the young man got his bicycle, she said, "Why don't you go ahead and I'll see you later." He then walked his bicycle the full length of the alley back to the main street. I walked along with him. His English was very limited and he did not say anything further. I had no idea where we were going. When we reached the main street he motioned to the back of his bicycle and said, "Get on." I straddled the back wheel and rode on a cargo platform about four inches wide. At that moment I thought, "I'm sixty years old. I have no idea who this man is. I don't know where we're going. What am I doing out here?"

He headed out into the bicycle traffic which is always heavy on Sunday afternoons. I held on to his waist, and even though I could not see where we were going, I could feel the struggle until the bike gained some momentum. We headed toward the underpass and going down hill I could feel him weaving around and through the bicycle traffic. Although I was not frightened, I made sure I kept my knees in. On the far side of the underpass we went uphill for about one hundred yards, and I could feel the extra effort that required. After about a quarter of a mile he turned into another alley, again crowded with free market vendors and then stopped in front of a shop.

We went in. On one side was a lady dispensing flour in bulk. She directed me to the other side where there was a cashier's window. I stood in a short line, and braced myself just a bit to retain my place in line. I laid a five yuan note on the counter and asked for two jin. (Two jin is about two pounds.) She asked me for my ration coupon. I said I did not have any. (*Mei you.*) She said, "Then you cannot have any flour." My young man shifted into gear and talked Chinese a mile-a-minute for some time. Finally the lady handed me two cards for the two *jin* and my change. When the young man saw my change he said something else. I did not catch it, but apparently he was concerned at the higher price I was being charged because I did not have the ration coupon. At that point the customer standing next to me pushed forward one of her ration coupons. The clerk took it, took back my change, re-figured it, and gave me the increased amount. The two *jin* of flour cost me fifty *fen*, or a little over a dime in United States currency equivalency.

I took the two cards to the lady dispensing flour. She said I would have to have my own bag. Fortunately Leona and I had purchased an acrylic cutting board in the alley earlier. I had been carrying it with me all this time, holding it with one hand while I was hanging on to the man's waist in front of me. The cutting board was in a sealed plastic package. I opened the package, took out the cutting board, and handed the bag to the lady. She filled it with two jin of flour and we were all set; almost.

"Get on," and we headed back through traffic. Now I was carrying a cutting board and a bag of flour. When the young man arrived opposite the university gate he stopped, I stood up, and as I was saying thank you, he was on his way. I don't even know his name.

Riding a Bicycle in China is a Contact Sport

The city buses in China are very crowded and very few people have access to an automobile. If we intended to go anywhere while we lived in China, we needed bicycles.

We walked to the Friendship Store where the better quality bikes are sold. They had about thirty bicycles, but only two different brands. China produces only two or three kinds of bicycles for the general populace. We were advised to buy the best quality and then we could more easily resell it to someone when we left. We each bought a Forever, made in Shanghai. None of the bicycles are **five speed** or **ten speed**; they are just two-speed, stop and go. Most of the bicycles are black. We felt fortunate that we found a maroon one for Leona.

Based on past bicycle experience in China, I also purchased pliers, screw driver, and a crescent wrench. This proved fortuitous. The following Sunday Leona's bicycle chain broke, and on the way to church my pedal fell off.

We wheeled our new bicycles out to the street, climbed on, and pedaled into the traffic. Once you have learned to ride a bicycle you never forget. Right? I used to ride a bike when I was a kid. Riding a bike is no problem. But here, the conditions are different; here, in China, riding a bicycle is a contact sport.

The first hazard for bicycle riding in China is sheer numbers. Major streets have bike lanes twenty five to thirty feet wide, but that space is filled, particularly during the rush hours, with bicycles. The population of China is over one billion and most of them ride bicycles. If any of them do not own a bicycle, they must be borrowing them just to ride them down town every weekend. You know what it is like to be in a sports stadium; put all those people on bicycles and call it Sunday in Nanchang. I have compared riding a bicycle on Sunday to skiing at Squaw Valley, California on a three day week-end.

When Leona and I ride together, she always wants me to follow her. This habit started five years ago in Nanjing when someone rode past her so closely, one day, that the straps from the bag he was carrying on his handle bars hooked over her handle bar and suddenly her front wheel turned ninety degrees, but she didn't. I was riding in front and didn't look back for another fifty feet. Leona was on the pavement. I was very surprised. She was very mad. I was very relieved because you cannot be that mad and be very seriously hurt, but you remember those incidents for a long time.

One day I was riding in traffic and felt a wheel rubbing against my back wheel. I turned my head and saw the young woman go down; at that point there was nothing I could do. Another time I turned left around a traffic guard rail and knocked someone down. Apparently he was trying to cut between me and the railing and I never saw him.

The way to ride a bike is simply to turn in the direction you are about to fall. When a child first learns to ride, it follows the path of a snake, turning from side to side to keep its balance. What do you do when bicycles are so close to you that you cannot turn? You strain to keep your balance; don't lean. We have an underpass near our university. Recently I was going down one end of the underpass and a young man went diagonally across my path. I leaned slightly to avoid him, but ran out of room, couldn't turn, and bailed out. My winter gloves saved me from the abrasive cement pavement, and fortunately other bicycles were able to avoid me. This occurrence is so common the man who cut me off never even looked back. Another time when I was going the opposite direction on the same underpass I was passing a bicycle when it suddenly swerved into me. My hand struck his brake handle, but both of us maintained our balance, and all I suffered was a slight bruise, again on a gloved hand.

I have witnessed dozens of bicycle accidents, but most of them have been *fender benders* because the bicycle traffic generally moves slowly. When two bicycles collide, one or both bicycles end up on the pavement, but no one else stops. There is no policeman, and no crowd. Everyone else just pedals around them and keeps on going. Oh, sometimes there is quite a "discussion" between the two that are involved, but since I do not understand enthusiastic Chinese "street" language, I cannot report what was said. I see the greatest potential for serious injury resulting from the mixing of trucks, buses, motorcycles and cars with the swarms of bicycles. The day before Christmas an interpreter and I were riding to the customs office to retrieve a package. The street was narrow and there was no bicycle lane. We had to ride down the middle of the street and got sandwiched between a municipal bus on our right and the oncoming truck traffic on our left. Even though the traffic was all moving slowly, it was a bit unnerving.

Motorized vehicles in China do have brakes, but they only use them as a last resort, whereas they use their horns constantly. If a car approaches an intersection filled with six bicycles and three pedestrians, it doesn't stop. The driver honks the horn, pulls into the other lane—the one for approaching traffic—and without even slowing down, goes around the people in the cross walk. One day I saw a car back out of an alley into a busy bike lane. A young woman cyclist stopped, but the backing car did not. When the car hit her bicycle she jumped off, and again there was no injury.

Bicycles are China's "family car" and consequently carry everything. I have seen five pound fish dangling from handle bars and the fish were still flopping. Bicycles carry live chickens, singly in their baskets, or hanging from the handle bars, or by the dozens in special crates on the back. I have seen dried fish, and a dozen little bamboo chairs in a fan-shaped pattern like the tail of a peacock. I saw a three-man plumbing crew. The first man carried three lengths of pipe about fifteen feet long. The second man carried a pipe threading tool, and the third man had a large pipe wrench—all on bicycles. People frequently carry propane tanks, bags of rice or flour, and decorated cakes. With this variety of cargo there is the occasional "oops," loose rice on the dirty street, oranges rolling under the traffic, shattered porcelain ware, etc. The cargo tricycles carry much heavier loads and they operate on the bicycle paths as well. I was following a load of wood paneling. The paneling was turned sideways and was cutting a wide swath through the heavy bicycle traffic. The driver had to swerve to avoid two middle school students coming from the other direction and the corner of his load of paneling caught the guard rail. It sounded like the *Titanic* hitting an iceberg as he ripped off about an inch strip from the bottom three sheets.

Riding bicycles in China is also a family affair. Wee ones are tied into wicker seats on the bar. Larger children, teen age friends, and even spouses frequently ride side saddle on the rack in back. Recently we saw a man stopped in the middle of bicycle traffic, standing next to his bicycle and shouting and shaking his three year old daughter who was riding on the back. Chinese parents are generally not physical when disciplining their children. We were so surprised by his aggressiveness that we stopped to see what was going on. He saw us stop and explained that his daughter was falling asleep. He had to wake her up so she wouldn't fall off the back.

I followed a young mother once who had a two year old riding on the back of her bicycle. The child was sound asleep, and had leaned forward, resting his head against his mother's back. Gradually the head and upper body would begin to sag to one side. The mother would then reach back and "hike" his head upright. In about fifty feet it would sag again, and she would hike it up again. I followed her for about three hikes.

Riding bicycles at night is another experience. In October Leona was in the hospital for three days. I visited her each evening and then would ride my bike home about 9:30. There is not much "night life" in a Chinese city so the traffic is light, but the streets are very dimly lit—maybe one light bulb every couple hundred feet. None of the bicycles have lights.

Cars run on their parking lights until the driver sees something; then the driver suddenly turns the headlights on, just long enough to blind you, then turns them off again. In addition to watching for cars, knowing they cannot see you, one has to watch for bicycles without lights, pedestrians, and road hazards. I have had to avoid loose bricks spilled on the street, and two inch cracks in the pavement. I have seen metal-framed holes in the cement about two feet wide and several inches deep; they must be part of the storm drain system. There is also an occasional open sewer hole in the middle of the street. One consolation, when one *drives* at night, there is no problem with falling asleep as there is in a car.

Nanchang has a lot of rain and that can create its problems too. Everyone carries a raincoat. People with small children have special raincoats with two hoods, one for the adult and another about chest high for the head of the little one riding in the wicker seat on the bar in front of him or her. We call them "kangaroo" rain coats. Nanchang is flat and the streets have poor drainage. When you ride through a puddle you lose your brakes. There are places where the standing water extends half way or two thirds of the way across the bike path. At those points everyone converges to the dry part. That gives you a choice between *suicide alley* and the *river route*.

When riding a bicycle in Nanchang beware of the Happy Birthday song. I was riding my bicycle in the downtown area one day. There was a lot of bicycle traffic, but it was a pleasant day, and my thoughts were drifting elsewhere. I became aware of music playing; it sounded something like the *Good Humor Truck* that use to ply our neighborhood in southern California tempting all the children to come out and buy ice cream. It was playing the Happy Birthday song. I didn't pay much attention. Suddenly I noticed all the people around me were steering over to the side of the street—some even jumping off their bicycles and climbing up on the two and three-step entrances to the little shops. What is going on? Too late! A tank truck came by spraying water out both sides, in order to clean the street. The initial blast comes out about eighteen inches high. Out about ten feet it hits the pavement, which is always filthy, and then splashes up again, spraying the now dirty water all over everything. I held my feet up, but could not avoid the spray. I have seen this same water truck several times. It really makes the cyclists scatter. So now, whenever I hear the Happy Birthday song I dash for cover too.

Riding Bicycles—Post Script

When Leona and I rode bicycles together, I rode about ten feet behind her in case she had any difficulties. I did not mind this role because it allowed me to observe the reactions of the bystanders. Whenever Leona approached, heads would turn and eyes would follow her course as she passed. At first I assumed the attention was prompted by her being a foreigner, a rare sight in Nanchang. But then I began analyzing the Chinese bicycle traffic. I saw men of all ages, but I saw only younger women. Very few older women ride bicycles in Nanchang. I later asked three of our men students aged thirty-five to forty-five if their wives rode bicycles. One said, "No," another said, "Sometimes," and the third said, "She is just learning." My wife is older than they are, and she frequently rode a bicycle.

Although Leona was a careful bicycle rider, she was not a strong rider, and whenever we approached a small hill or steep slope I would ride up next to her, put a hand on the small of her back and help her up the incline. In Nanchang one of the steep slopes was the underpass.

Early in July the weather had turned hot and muggy and our clothes began to mold in the closet. Leona is allergic to molds, and she had developed a shortness of breath. The four mile round trip to church that morning had been a struggle for her, and now we just had to climb that last steep incline from the underpass and we would be back at the university. We were in heavy bicycle traffic. We swerved to pass a cargo tricycle, leaving a safe margin of a couple feet. That proved our downfall. Another cargo tricycle rider, trying to maintain his speed going up the hill tried to go through that two foot space. To gain more room he cut diagonally in front of Leona. His back wheel hit her front wheel causing her to fall against me and we both fell in a tangled pile on the curb. We both yelled at the rider. The cargo tricycle stopped and the man came back to see if we were hurt. We were shaken, but not hurt—we were not aware of some of the bruises until later—so I waved the man on.

We picked up our bicycles. I straightened Leona's handle bars. We parked both bicycles against the curb, Leona's on the outside, while we stood on the sidewalk a moment to regain our confidence. The Sunday traffic was heavy and included the usual mix: bicycles, pull carts, and cargo tricycles.

A cargo tricycle is pedal driven. It has one wheel in front, and a cargo box in back with a wheel on each side. The wheels are slightly larger than a bicycle, but heavier in order to support the heavy loads these tricycles carry. I refer to them as the Chinese pick-up.

We had stood there for less than a minute when another cargo tricycle rider, pedaling hard to maintain his speed on the slope, misjudged his distance as he went by us. He was carrying a raggedy load of bags and rags and something stuck out just far enough to hook on Leona's handle bar. His momentum jerked Leona's parked bicycle into the lane of traffic directly in front of a young Chinese woman. She could not avoid the abrupt obstacle so she and her bicycle went sprawling on top of Leona's bike.

The bicycle traffic never stops, and neither did the cargo tricycle rider. I watched him until he disappeared beyond the top of the hill. The Chinese woman was unhurt. Leona's bicycle seat was badly lacerated, but she was still standing on the sidewalk and therefore not physically involved, but rather unsettled emotionally.

I grabbed Leona's bike and said, "Let's get out of here." Leona responded, "Let's go!" I was referring to the underpass, but at that moment Leona was thinking, "From China!"

The English Corner[3]

It was Sunday afternoon. We could see forty or fifty Chinese, old and young, male and female, standing in a corner of Gulou Park. We walked toward the group and then stopped. I was immediately surrounded, and Leona, standing twenty feet away, was surrounded by her own group.

"Where are you from?"

---

[3] In Gulou (Drum Tower) Park, Nanjing, in 1986.

"Have you been to China before?"

"Tell us about your city."

The questions became more difficult.

"What are some of the differences between China and the U. S. A.?"

"Do the young people have difficulty in getting along with their parents?"

"How much does a motor bike cost?"

"Tell us about colleges in America."

I had heard about the English Corner, but I had never experienced one. Apparently they have English corners in parks in Beijing and several other cities. It is a very non-structured activity. Everyone who wants to talk English goes to that particular location every Sunday afternoon at 3:30. (In Nanchang the English Corner was on Sunday morning.)

My wife and I were invited by one of the university teachers who is active in the university English Club. Most of the people in the park, however, were not students, but townspeople. We rode our bicycles about a mile to the park, walked twenty feet into the crowd, and the show started. The people surrounded me, standing three or four deep. Several asked questions and the rest listened. My space was limited to perhaps twelve inches; I had just enough room to turn about thirty degrees, occasionally.

Prompted by their view of America gleaned from the Voice of America, the British Broadcasting Corporation, and the required political studies classes, they asked questions on the following topics: the excessive number of traffic accidents, why we are spending so much money on Star Wars, do we all have weapons in our homes and isn't that dangerous, the function of political parties, and why Americans are moving all the time. They are honestly interested in American culture because they also asked, "How many square meters are in the average home," "Can you buy a used car very cheap," "Do eighteen year old's have difficulty finding jobs," "Why do so many Americans believe in God?" (No one said the questions would be easy.) They wanted to know which universities were best in mathematics, and the difference between an M.D. and a Ph.D. in medicine (apparently some Chinese students study for Ph.D.'s in medicine.)

Some people are very nervous when they travel in a communist country because of the fear that party members will be watching them and listening to what they say. If one feels that people are spying on you, do not go to an English Corner. One has no idea whom he or she is talking to; they are all strangers.

At 4:30 our Chinese escort rescued us and said that

perhaps it was time for us to return to our university. We were highly stimulated, but tired and relieved to go. I had the feeling that they would have stayed there as long as we did, regardless of the hour.

As we were riding home my wife asked how my English discussion went. I said, "That was not a discussion; it was a press conference."

Medical Examination Mania
or
"We Don't Want You to Die While You Are Here."

Last Tuesday morning there was a knock on the door. It was our *waiban* (foreign affairs officer), and we could tell that something was very important. He handed me a three page handwritten statement in English and asked me to read it. To share it with Leona I read it aloud. The statement was addressed to all six of the foreign teachers. It said:

> None of your medical papers are complete. You must all take E.C.G., chest X-ray, and serodiagnosis. We will have a car to pick you up. Be at the guest house gate Friday morning at 7:45.

We were shocked, not only by the request, but by the peremptory nature of the announcement. In preparation for teaching in China we had taken comprehensive physical examinations in the United States including a battery of blood tests. We had even paid sixty-five dollars extra for a special HIV-aids test (which seemed of special importance to the Chinese government.) In California we had, however, taken the tyne skin test instead of a chest X-ray and we had skipped the electrocardiogram, feeling that should not be necessary just to teach school. We had then hand carried our medical forms to China and had presented them to the *waiban's* office (Foreign Affairs Office). Now they were telling us to repeat the blood tests and were still insisting on the chest X-rays and the electrocardiogram.

I told the waiban, "We are willing to take an E.C.G. and a chest X-ray, but we had complete blood tests in the United States including the HIV-aids test and we will not repeat those tests."

The waiban said, "You will have to talk with my superiors."

I talked with the other four Americans. They were sponsored by the American based E.L.I.C., English Language Institute in China. They said their sponsors had an agreement, "No additional medical tests after arriving in China." They telephoned their Hong Kong office and were directed to adhere to their contract and refuse any further medical tests. To present a common front I wrote a letter to the Foreign Affairs Office saying we had had our physical examinations, we had sent them in with our applications, the Chinese authorities had accepted our applications, and we did not feel we should have to take additional tests. If they wanted to discuss this further, they could call our superior, Ting Yen Ren, in Nanjing.

The next afternoon the waiban told the ELIC lead teacher that "they could stay in China." We hoped that meant us too, and hoped the case was closed.

On Tuesday morning the *waiban* told me, "I have talked with the Amity Office in Nanjing (our sponsoring body), and you must take your physicals."

"You mean the E.C.G. and the chest X-ray?"

"Yes."

"We'd be happy to."

"A car will pick you up at 7:45 on Thursday."

We were reluctant to take further blood tests because of our concern regarding China's medical sterile technique. In case we needed any injections while we were there, we had even been supplied with hypodermic needle kits by our sponsor.

There are several hospitals in Nanchang. Being foreigners we were taken to the Number One hospital for our physical examinations. We waited for forty-five minutes in the waiting room, long enough to survey the scene. The walls were painted an institutional green and shabby white, a rather common decor in China. The exposed plumbing ran up the wall. From one of the pipes, suspended by a string and held together by a large clip, was a sheaf of papers. The wooden floor had been painted at one time, but now bare wood peeked out in several places. The four inch hole in the center of the ceiling was partially covered by a three-inch ceiling mount for a light. The plastic vase on the table held a bouquet of plastic flowers. In contrast to an American hospital waiting room there were no magazines, not even any old ones.

A man wearing a white lab coat was sitting at a desk; he had a stethoscope in his pocket, so we assumed he was a doctor. He asked us, "Where are you from?" We said that we were from California. That was the entire conversation. After some minutes the doctor left. About five minutes later the doctor returned, this time carrying a saw like what we used to use to cut down a Christmas tree at one of those "Choose and Cut" Christmas tree farms, except this one was very rusty. The doctor put the saw in his desk drawer. Somehow, this made Leona very nervous.

In China the people in charge never explain anything in advance. You wait until they are ready; then you go where they take you. We were escorted outside, across the courtyard to another building, up the stairs, and then down a long dimly lit hallway. The hallway was very narrow because of a long row of cabinets on one side and a row of chairs on the other. Our faith in the technology of Chinese medicine was tarnished just as the walls and floors were tarnished.

We stopped at the entrance to the chest X-ray room. While we were waiting they carried in an old man lying on an army field stretcher. They set the stretcher on the floor. The old man stared at us with vacant eyes; his head was immobile. A Chinese soldier dressed in a PLA uniform walked in behind us. A frightened young man, dressed in baggy, rumpled clothing, was handcuffed to his wrist.

Someone called Leona's name and she stepped into the room. They took her to the far wall and positioned her against a plate. Everyone walked out into the hallway and the door was closed. The X-ray controls were in the hallway. Someone pulled a lever—zap, and we all went back into the room to see if Leona were still alive. Then it was my turn. We waited a few minutes in the hallway for our film to be developed. They announced that our chests were "normal."

When we returned to the reception room there were seven young women in white lab coats and two young men. They were taking blood samples from six young men at one end of the room and doing electrocardiograms at the other. I unbuttoned my shirt, took off my shoes, and climbed onto the bed, the same bed that had been used by everyone else. Then it was Leona's turn—in public. A woman in a white lab coat slid two electrodes under her blouse, put two more on her wrists, and one on her ankle. They turned on the machine.

As the machine operated, it printed out a recording tape showing the heart beat. A nurse was holding the recording machine in her lap. Someone tapped her on the shoulder;

she had a telephone call. She laid the recorder down and left. Another nurse picked it up, adjusted some dials, and watched it. I looked over her shoulder. Leona's pattern was a flat line. "Oh, no!" The nurse turned some more dials and a nice pattern developed. "Whew!" We both passed!

They still had some questions concerning our blood test information on the health forms we brought from the United States. I pointed to the data, but they have little faith in an American doctor's signature; they want it stamped by something governmental like a county hospital. I reassured them the blood tests were done by the Sacramento laboratory and that Sacramento was our state capital. That gave them more confidence in our test results. They still wanted assurance that we had had an HIV test. (They could not do an HIV test in Nanchang; they would have had to send our blood sample to Shanghai.) They were finally satisfied with our blood tests and said we could leave.

On the way home I asked the waiban if all the Chinese teachers had had electrocardiograms. He said, "No." But it sure seemed important that we had them.

Hospital Hospitality

On Tuesday, October 9, Leona developed a sore throat. On Wednesday morning she felt worse, but decided to teach her seven-thirty to nine-thirty class anyway. Right after class I went with her to the university health clinic. To help with the medical terminology we took an interpreter.

When we entered the doctor's office there was no waiting room, and no chairs provided for the patients who were waiting. We stepped just inside the door and joined a half dozen Chinese standing against the wall waiting their turn. From this vantage point we could not only survey the room, but also watch each patient being examined. In China, where there is a population of 1.1 billion people, privacy is not a high priority. What we saw, however, did not raise our confidence level regarding Chinese medicine.

The doctors' office was large, perhaps twenty by twenty. The cement floor was bare. The cement walls had an institutional green wainscot and dingy white paint above it. There was a cement sink in the corner holding a mop. Against the wall next to the sink was the doctor's bicycle.

There were two doctors, a man and a woman, sitting at desks on opposite sides of the room. The doctors were dressed in white lab coats and each wore a stethoscope. Next to each desk was a small, four legged stool for the patient.

When it was Leona's turn, she walked forward and took her place on the stool. We all stood and watched. Our interpreter described the symptoms. The doctor thumbed through a batch of tongue depressors in a cup on his desk, selected one and looked at her throat. Then he felt her pulse. Then he wrote out a prescription. It cost us about forty-five cents to have the prescription filled. The medicine included some little packets of powder that resembled ovaltine, some pills for anti-inflammation, little yellow pills to suck, and vitamin C. It is terribly frustrating to be in a foreign country when you are sick and not to know what medicine you are taking because no one can translate the medical names into terms you understand. Because of the low concentration of chemicals in Chinese pills, she was required to take about thirty-five pills each day. She began taking them all as prescribed immediately.

Leona's condition worsened during the night. At daylight I gave her an orange and she vomited. At noon she tried soup and 7-Up and could not keep that down either. I sent for the doctor from the clinic.

When a foreigner is sick, everyone becomes concerned. When the doctor arrived he was accompanied by the Director of the Training Center where we taught, and his two administrative assistants. Our house manager, Mrs. Li, was also there. While the four men stood at Leona's bedside conferring as to whether she should go to the hospital, Mrs. Li held her hand and massaged her wrists. Leona asked if the hospital had a western toilet. They assured her that it did. The decision was made, and they sent for a car.

I assumed the stay in the hospital would be overnight, so I got down her little bag and threw in a nightgown, her robe, a tooth brush, a book, etc.

When the van arrived at the hospital we were taken to the same reception room where we had had our physical examinations the previous month. After a brief wait I registered, paid five yuan (equivalent to about one dollar in American money) and we were taken upstairs to a private room with a private bathroom and a western style toilet.

A woman doctor came in and said she wanted to begin her intravenous procedure and to take a blood test. We told her she could begin the intravenous injections, but asked if she would wait until tomorrow to see if the blood test was necessary. She assured us that they only used "one-time" needles. It was ironic. After we had fought so hard just a month before to avoid retaking blood tests, we had returned to the same hospital and blood tests were necessary anyway.

Two women brought in a metal cot and started setting it up. I asked, "Who is that for?"

They responded, "For you!"

I quickly said, "No, no, I'm not staying."

They asked, "Why not?"

I turned to our interpreter and asked, "Do they expect me to take care of Leona?—to feed her?—or. . .?"

"No, the hospital will take care of her, but perhaps you need to talk to her."

I said that I did not think that was necessary and furthermore, no one had suggested that I was supposed to stay so I had not brought anything.

Our interpreter, Xiao Yao, one of the administrative assistants from the Training Center, said, "Then I will stay."

That wasn't quite what I had in mind. He then suggested we ask two of our women students to stay. I quickly agreed. Our women students were happy to have the opportunity to take care of their foreign teacher. Two came that evening and others came in relay shifts and stayed at Leona's bedside the entire time she was in the hospital. They slept on that little cot, one curled up at each end. They massaged her, rubbed aromatic oil in her hair, brought her water or a wet towel, and kept her company.

Xiao Yao asked, "What about supper?"

I asked, "Doesn't the hospital provide meals?"

He said, "It is too late this afternoon to make arrangements for tonight's meal, but the hospital will provide meals beginning tomorrow."

I asked Xiao Gan, the other administrative assistant from the Training Center, to go out and get some noodles. At that point Leona said she was thirsty. There was a thermos of boiled water in the room, but no cup.

"Xiao Gan, bring back a cup also."

Xiao Gan was gone a long time. Finally he returned, carrying a pot of hot noodles on his bicycle. The pot looked familiar; he had gone back to the Guest House, and had our cook prepare the noodles. He had also brought our cups and silverware.

The woman doctor returned and rolled in a stand with tubes and bottles for Leona's intravenous injections. She hooked up a large bottle of glucose and saline solution and placed two more bottles on the night stand. The needle looked huge; she reiterated that they only used "one-time" needles. While Leona was receiving the fluid, another woman doctor gave her an injection in the other arm.

It takes a couple of hours for the intravenous bottle to empty. While it was still dripping into Leona's right arm, three staff people came in to give Leona a blood test. (So much for waiting until tomorrow.) There were three staff people—I forgot to mention that this was a teaching hospital. One pricked her finger and made a slide. Then another inserted a needle, but could not find a vein. She wiggled the needle around, pulled it out, and tried a couple more times. I was watching and wincing every time she stuck the needle into a different spot. She then switched to the other arm, slightly below the intravenous needle, but after a couple tries, returned to the first arm and stuck the needle into the back of her hand—I winced again—and slowly, ever so slowly, she filled a vial with blood.

A male doctor came in and listened to Leona's chest. He found an area in her lungs that was noisy. He handed the stethoscope to a young woman who had accompanied him so that she could hear the noise. The hospital is connected with the medical university, so I assumed she was in training. The doctor analyzed the lung sound as a lung infection and directed one of the others to replace the second and third intravenous bottles with one containing an antibiotic. They also gave Leona an expectorant cough syrup. It was at this moment that Xiao Gan returned with the freshly cooked noodles. Leona's appetite, if it ever existed, had long since vanished.

Xiao Gan and I rode our bicycles back to the hospital the next morning at seven-fifteen. The doctor came in to see how Leona was doing. She looked brighter and felt much better. I told the doctor we wanted to check out and go home. The doctor wanted to keep her in the hospital. Chinese patients stay in Chinese hospitals longer than patients do in the United States, (four weeks for a broken leg, for example), and Chinese doctors are particularly careful with foreign patients.

The doctor wanted Leona to have a chest X-ray. (We had had chest X-rays just three weeks earlier as part of our physical examinations for teaching.)

Leona was pretty weak, but we helped her up, put on her robe and a coat and our two students walked on either side, helping her go down the stairs, across the same courtyard to the same building where we had gone three weeks before. We climbed the same stairs and went down the same dimly lit hallway.

This time I noticed there was a bare, low wattage light bulb about every thirty feet, and the walls needed a coat of paint. Against the walls on either side were bags and boxes further restricting the space in the narrow corridor. We stopped at a room with a heavy insulated door, the same room we were in before. Leona was able to sit on a little stool while we waited for about ten minutes.

While we were waiting, two men carried a stretcher down the hall, and set it on the floor near us. A badly injured older man lay on the stretcher, watching us with staring eyes. The whole experience seemed like a re-run from the previous month, but this time Leona was sick and everything seemed more significant.

When it was Leona's turn they took her in, had her stand with her chest against the wall and then everyone went out into the hallway, leaving Leona in there by herself. As weak as she was she stood alone. I wondered how they would deal with the old man on the stretcher. They closed the door, threw the switch, and we all went back inside to rescue our patient. We waited in the hallway for another ten minutes. Leona had the only stool. The X-ray results were satisfactory; Leona had passed, so we all returned to her hospital room. The doctor said she had a bronchial infection and she could not go home. We immediately asked, "Then how about tomorrow?"

The doctor agreed to "Tomorrow afternoon."

The nurse came in and asked if Leona wanted the intravenous again or two injections. Leona chose the intravenous, but they still gave her one injection—it was a huge vial, about eight ounces, and after the needle was in, the nurse slowly pushed the plunger, emptying the solution into the blood stream. Leona said that really hurt. When she was finished, she then hooked up the intravenous drip again. At that point, you guessed it, "What do you want for lunch?"

The morning team of two more of our women students, Mrs. Yu, and Mrs. Gu, arrived about eight o'clock. The night shift, Mrs. Wang and Mrs. Cao left about nine-thirty. I went back to the university to teach Leona's morning class.

In the afternoon, after *xiu xi*, (the afternoon rest period), I told the Training Center I was going back to the hospital. They felt I should not go alone, so they asked one of the clerks to go with me. I thought this was strange since I was used to riding all over town by myself. I allowed the clerk to lead, but as we got near the hospital I had to tell her where to turn. Then the guard at the hospital gate stopped her and would not let her in until I stepped forward and said, "She's with me." So much for having an escort.

Leona and our two students gave us a cheery greeting. Leona was doing fine, but couldn't wait to tell me, "Guess what they did after you left?"

"An E.C.G.?"

"Yes."

The Chinese are very protective of their foreign guests.

Just before supper a group of men walked in; they were all of our male students. They were cheery, but concerned about their foreign teacher. They stayed just a few minutes and then excused themselves. I have no idea how they got there. They did not have their bicycles in Nanchang. There is no direct bus. Did they all walk?

Xiao Yao, the administrative assistant, arrived, bringing a bouquet of roses from the Training Center. In urban areas Chinese live mostly in apartment houses without gardens. Flowers of any kind are scarce. We were touched. He requested an itemized bill from the hospital so he could have a check prepared for the following day. He also asked Leona about her medical insurance.

The senior doctor came in, checked Leona, and told us Leona could go home the following day. He spoke very little English, but through our interpreter he said that there was still a rattle in Leona's lungs, but since we were insistent, we could leave the next day. We were excited. We were ready.

Before the doctor left, a young doctor came in and through an interpreter announced that the previous day's blood tests indicated there was sugar in her blood.

"Have you ever had diabetes?"

Leona said, "No."

"We must keep you in the hospital longer so that we can take more blood tests to make sure."

Leona and I both responded excitedly, "Of course there's sugar in her blood. What did you expect? You're dripping glucose intravenously into one arm while you're drawing blood out of the other."

We were furious. The doctor did not speak much English. Either he was not convinced or he did not understand us. I stated it more emphatically, "There will be no more blood tests."

We were thinking, "Leona didn't have diabetes symptoms when she came into the hospital. She had a bronchial infection and was dehydrated from vomiting." The hospital had corrected those problems with an anti-biotic and intravenous fluids. We had put up with a chest X-ray, blood tests, and an electrocardiogram that we thought were superfluous. Now "Enough was enough!" We wanted to go home.

The young doctor asked, "Where is your interpreter?" I gave him the Training Center phone number and fortunately Xiao Gan answered. They talked a long time. Then I asked for the phone, and I told Xiao Gan that we were not willing to take any more blood tests. I told him Leona had been treated for the symptoms she had had and now we wanted to go home tomorrow. Xiao Gan said he would try to convince the doctor. I gave the phone back to the doctor and after several minutes of conversation, he hung up. He turned to me and said, "Thank you," and left. Had we won? We did not know.

When I left the hospital Leona asked me to take home all of the bulky items she had brought. The only things she kept was what we could carry on one bicycle. She said, "If they won't release us tomorrow, we might just go anyway!" I knew she was feeling better.

The next morning the nurse wheeled in the apparatus. We wondered, "Was this for a blood test?"

"No, it was for one final intravenous injection."

Leona was nervous. Why have another injection if her sugar was already too high? It is frustrating not to be able to communicate with your doctor. Two of our students were constantly at Leona's bedside. Whenever a doctor came into the room he would talk to the students in Chinese. (They were thirty-five to forty years old and all had their own families.) Then the doctor would leave.

We would ask the students, "What did he say?"

Their response, "We can't explain it in English."

Another problem developed from this lack of communication. Leona felt that her original vomiting may have been an allergic reaction to some of her medicine. So when pills were presented to her in the hospital she wanted to know what they were. Their response, "They are anti-inflammation medicine."

Leona asked for a more specific explanation, but none was forthcoming. She said, "I do not want to take the medicine unless I know what it is."

The response was, "If she won't take her medicine, we'll give it to her intravenously." Also, "She may not go home yet because she would have no facilities for intravenous injections."

Finally someone "found" a printout in English explaining the chemical content and purpose for the bottle of pills and the "problem" disappeared.

That afternoon the Training Center van arrived. I wanted to take Leona downstairs to the van, but was told, "You can't check out until you pay the bill and it hasn't been made up yet."

While we were waiting we thought we could at least go to the pharmacy and get the prescription filled. It was closed; it would open after the *xiu xi* rest period.

We waited for another thirty minutes. "The bill is not ready. You can go on home and pay the bill tomorrow."

Leona was still pretty weak, but she was so relieved just to be home. The hospital bill for two nights including the doctors' services, blood test, chest X-ray, electro-cardiogram, oxygen, and all medications was equivalent to one hundred seventy-five dollars, in U. S. currency. There was a separate bill for meals—six dollars.

Leona's final assessment: "It was worth every penny of it."

What'd He Say?[4]

When you live in a foreign country without knowing the native language, your primary contact with your students, colleagues, friends, and everyone you meet, is in their second language, English. Dealing with people in their second language leads to some frustrations, but also to a lot of giggles.

We were staying in a hotel in Shanghai. We asked at the desk, "What time is breakfast?"

The response, "The dining room will be open at 8:00."

We are early risers, so we had to kill time, waiting for the dining room to open at eight o'clock. Finally, right at eight o'clock, we walked into the dining room. They were just closing their doors. I asked again, "What time is breakfast?"

They said, "The dining room is open **till** 8:00."

While Leona was in the hospital there were always at least two of our women students at her bedside. They were very concerned about their foreign teacher and very sensitive to her needs and her well-being. The doctors were also concerned about their foreign patient and different ones would walk in, look at Leona, then look at me, and never say a word. Then they would turn to our two Chinese students and talk very excitedly for several minutes in Chinese.

Our Chinese students would respond with their own excited remarks. All of our women students had children, the younger ones had one child according to Chinese policy, and some of the older women had several children.

---

[4] Written for *The Lodi News Sentinel* while the author was still in Nanchang, 1990/91.

Having had the experience as mothers and of raising their own families, they also expressed their own opinions to the doctor regarding Leona's health. Then the doctor would leave. Leona and I would turn to our two students and excitedly ask, "What'd he say?" Their casual response was, "He asked if you were feeling better?" Somehow we did not feel that translation captured the whole conversation.

We were watching a movie in a Chinese theater. We did not catch the title of the film and had no advance knowledge of the plot. We were simply informed, in honor of Teacher Recognition Day, we will take you to a movie. In 1986 we were taken to "First Blood," a Rambo movie, for Teacher Recognition Day, so we knew what to expect.

The theater was packed and we could hear the audience respond with oohs, and aahs, gasps and tsks. We tried to follow the story line by watching the action, but were constantly turning to our Chinese companion with, "What'd he say?" It was an action-packed story, and we at least wanted to know who the "good guys or gals" were.

When a character wearing a white uniform was giving orders to a group of men, we asked, "Who is that?" "He is a policeman." We thought, of course, white uniform—white hat, he must be a good guy. As we watched, however, the policeman murdered a witness in close-up living color, accepted a bribe, and did other treacherous acts. Gradually we identified another character who, although violent, appeared to be on the side of justice, honesty, and mercy. In the final scene, the "good guy" that we had identified, was stood before a firing squad and shot. We did not understand. Our companion's simple explanation, "Oh, that was before Liberation (1949). There was no justice then."

Speaking English as a second language can also produce its problems with Chinese teachers of English. Our students had been teaching English for ten to fifteen years, but they had had limited contact with native speakers and their oral skills were very minimal.

One of our male students received a phone call from his wife requesting urgently that he come home. He left a note for us stating he would return in three days and caught a bus for the eight to ten hour trip home. We were interested in knowing what the emergency was so we asked our best student if he knew why Mr. Deng had had to go home so suddenly. He said, "His house was stolen."

We thought about that for awhile, but continued to ask other students. Finally we found out that he had had a burglary. Later we learned that the burglary had occurred the previous April, six months earlier, but the police had just gained some new evidence, and the wife thought her husband might be able to help solve the crime.

One day one of our female students was absent. We asked the other students where she was. In China people live in such close quarters that everyone knows everyone else's business. We were told that our student had gone to the hospital where her eighteen year old son was having surgery. We asked the purpose of the surgery.

"What is wrong with her son?"

The reply, "He was born with three waists."

We did not believe that and pursued the matter further. One of our students insisted that that was correct. She put her hands on her waist to demonstrate. We questioned her again. She spelled waist, "*W a i s t.*" I had visions of a very tall boy with one waist above the other, or would he be very fat?

"How will the surgery help?" "What will they do?"

She said, "They will remove one."

I wondered how you would cut off someone's waist and what would happen to the other two. Finally we asked a doctor to talk to our student and find out what was happening. After talking back and forth in Chinese for several minutes the doctor told us, "The woman's son is having a kidney removed."

A Routine Ride to the Park[5]

After nine days of rain, March 7 broke bright and clear. It had been windy, wet and cold, but today was hot and humid. We took advantage of the beautiful day and went bicycle riding. We stopped at a little shop and bought a *jin* of red sugar (a *jin* is about a pound, and brown sugar is called red sugar in China.) The clerk had already weighed out the sugar into one *jin* plastic bags. I put the bag in my waist pack since Chinese stores do not use paper sacks.

The traffic was heavy as usual. It's a little intimidating just to cross the street. We first had to cross the bike path filled with hundreds of bicycles mixed with pull carts, pedestrians, and cargo pedi-tricycles. Then we wheeled our bikes out into the street. While standing in the cross walk one is still not safe. On-coming traffic just blow their horns, swerve around you, and keep right on going. As far as we can tell, no one has the right-of-way. Once we got into the bike lane on the far side, we followed our usual pattern, "just go with the flow."

We soon turned off the main street and went past the neighborhood landfill where trucks were dumping their refuse, and about a dozen scavengers were sifting through the waste, looking for treasures. I was amused by an old sow—it must have been four hundred pounds—and unattended, that was also working its claim.

Beyond the landfill we came to a large, beautiful lake and a pretty tree-lined bike path. On the lake were racing shells propelled by single rowers and by teams of rowers. We passed a large apartment house about five stories high. Each apartment had a small balcony with rows of potted plants. Since the sun was shining everyone had their wash suspended from bamboo poles outside their windows. People call this colorful array of laundry "The All Nations Flag." The apartment house was surrounded by a compound and a perimeter security wall with two gates, a

---

[5] Written for *The Galt Herald* and published in March 1991.

large one for vehicles and a small one for pedestrians and bicycles.

A little farther on we saw an apartment house under construction. The design was familiar, reinforced cement columns, prefab cement sections for the floors, and bricks to fill in the open spaces with non-bearing walls. There was a large cement mixer pouring cement into a wheelbarrow. A man then shoveled the cement into buckets. Each workman then picked up two buckets of cement with hooks that dangled from each end of his bamboo carry pole, and carried them to the building. There was a steady stream of full buckets, bouncing, sagging, as the spring of the bamboo matched the swing of their steps, and a return stream of empty buckets swinging jauntily. Nearby there was a truck loaded with bricks. There were two bamboo ramps from the truck bed to the ground. Workmen with bamboo poles walked up one ramp and down the other. The ones going up were light and sauntering; the ones going down loaded and slightly bouncing as their grappling hooks held ten bricks fore and aft. China has built a lot of new apartment houses in the last forty years. To keep pace with their growing population, they will need to repeat this scene again and again.

We got back on our bicycles and proceeded down the bike path. Soon we saw a small cemetery, at least there were twenty-five to thirty headstones each placed on a dirt mound three or four feet high. The official policy in China today requires cremation, but there are some burial sites tucked away here and there.

We continued for another mile around the lake. On the opposite side we passed fish ponds about an acre in size. One had been partially drained and a half dozen men were wading waist deep in water while holding up a long fish net. We could see them splashing, driving fish in front of them and eighteen inch fish jumping out of the water before them.

We arrived at a park located along the lake. We had never been there before, so we paid our five *mao* (that is equivalent to U.S. $.10) for both of us, and went in. It was a large park and very pretty. There were many trees, although many of them were dormant this time of year. We watched groups of visitors ride the tilt-a-whirl and the airplane swings and shoot in the shooting gallery. There was also a mono-rail. The track was in an oval shape about one hundred fifty yards long and elevated about ten feet above the ground. We watched the cars. They seemed to move a short distance, and then stop. Then they would proceed a little further, and then stop. Then they would move forward, going very slowly, and then stop. It took us some time to figure out what was going on. The mono-rail cars were pedal driven.

As we left the park we saw a man wheeling his bicycle and leading a huge water buffalo. Another water buffalo, about half grown, was trotting to keep up. Water buffalo are so big, but apparently very docile. People lead them with a rope the size of a clothes line.

The rest of the ride back was routine. We passed the usual pull carts. They carry incredible loads. We have seen them haul a dozen burlap bags filled with grain, or fifteen sacks of cement, re-bar, pipe, or pre-fab cement slabs. We have also seen cargo tricycles with a sofa and two stuffed chairs, or several pieces of office furniture. There were men and women with bamboo carry-poles carrying buckets, baskets, or bundles. There were streets lined with little shops, with shelves filled with goods, although there is not great variety, and hundreds of customers everywhere. But we saw these sights every day.

A Funny Thing Happened on the Way to the...University[6]

Nanchang, China, a city of one million, had about twenty-five American teachers scattered among a dozen colleges and universities. We all knew each other and most

[6] *The Galt Herald*, March 1991.

of us got together each Saturday for a potluck lunch and a chance for fellowship. One Saturday we went to the Railroad/Communications University. The university was in the suburbs on the other side of the river, too far for bicycles, so five of us from Jiangxi Teachers' University requested a school car. With the luxury of going by car we took more things than we would have taken on our bicycles. I had a large cardboard box filled with gifts for the occasion. Leona carried a deep frying pan filled with eggplant ratatouille, our contribution for the potluck. The other three Americans had similar items.

Since all of us are used to driving in the United States, we are used to watching the road when other people drive. That gets scary in China. For them driving is a continuous game of chicken, and the honking of horns is constant. After a while, however, we all settled down to a comfortable ride and enjoyed the sights. When we got to within half a mile of our destination, we came to some road construction. Workmen were rebuilding an overpass over a railroad track. Our driver stopped, got out, and talked with the workmen. No, he could not drive through the construction area. We had to get out and walk the rest of the way. We must have looked like a group of gypsies, the way the workmen watched all of us, carrying our boxes and pans of food. We had to climb down a slippery bank, walk across a train track, and then up the other side. Unfortunately, there was a long freight train sitting on the tracks, blocking our way. We all stopped; now what shall we do? Then we noticed several Chinese people crawling under the freight train. One young man was even dragging his bicycle under the train. So we all got down on our hands and feet; I was carrying/dragging my big box, and Leona was still carrying her frying pan of eggplant ratatouille. We had to keep low because the undercarriage of a freight train is black and dirty. We all wondered what on earth we were doing, but with minimal smudges, we made it to the other side and scrambled up the bank. We brushed off the dirt the best that we could, took a picture of ourselves, and quarter of a mile to the Railroad/Communications University. We told our American host at the University about our cross country trek and she was quite surprised. "Why that overpass has been like that for eight months; we thought every driver in town knew that!"

Reflecting back on this experience the events seemed to unfold quite naturally, but we would never have crawled under a freight train in Sacramento—only in China; and then, only *after the tour bus left*.

Chapter III

Good Morning Class

I was teaching English conversation to a class of middle-aged Chinese students in Nanchang when the following exchange took place.

"There is a popular saying in America, 'Everyone talks about the weather, but no one can do anything about it.' To better prepare you for everyday conversation, today's vocabulary lesson will be about the weather."

"Here in Nanchang the weather is very humid. Our first word will be *humidity*."

A student asks, "What's humidity?"

"Humidity is moisture in the air."

A student asks, "What's moisture?"

I looked around and spotted several drops of water on my desk top. I pointed to the spot on my desk and asked, "What's that?"

A forty year old student in the front desk squinted at the place I was pointing and said, "Dirt."

I thought a minute; then took my ever-present cup of tea and poured a little on my desk. I asked, "What's that?"

The same student responded brightly, "Tea."

The weather is still humid in Nanchang, but I am afraid that some of my students may never know.

Chinese education is teacher centered. The teacher carefully prepares a lesson and presents it to his/her class. The students listen, take notes, and learn the material in preparation for the next examination. The body of material is closely prescribed. The students are expected to over-learn it, memorizing much of the content. The junior middle and senior middle school classes (equivalent to junior high and high school classes in the United States) are large, averaging about sixty students, and discussion is limited. Students do not ask any questions beyond the stated lesson; they do not want to embarrass the teacher by asking a question beyond his/her preparation.

Westerners question China's stress on memorization, but Chinese children, beginning in the first grade, start memorizing Chinese characters. The Chinese language is not based on an alphabet. Students must memorize individual characters, perhaps ten thousand by the culmination of their senior middle school.

Traditionally, teachers had been held in high esteem in China until the Cultural Revolution. The Ten Chaotic Years, as the Chinese call the period from 1966 to 1976, was anti-intellectual, and millions of teachers and other intellectuals were sent to the countryside to be "re-educated" by performing menial tasks.

For a writing assignment I asked a class of college teachers to describe a class or a class period that had been memorable to them. One of the essays relates to a student's teaching experience during the Cultural Revolution:

> In 1976, the chaotic year, when I was teaching in a middle school in Inner Mongolia, I had the most unbearable experience as a teacher. One day when the bell was ringing, I entered the classroom. As soon as I was standing in front of the class, a murmur occurred. In spite of that, I began to explain the text and dared not stop, for I knew if I stopped, I could not begin again. The whole class would speak and I would not be heard. But the murmur turned into a louder voice and the voice became louder and louder. Suddenly, *pang!* A desk was

> turned upside down. A girl was pushed down on the ground by a stout boy. He kicked her on her back insanely. Before I could go over to stop him, the whole class stood up. Some whistled, some laughed, some jumped about, some yelled, some pounded their hands on the desks. The classroom was full of noise. I pushed the boy aside and pulled the girl up. Then I went back to the blackboard and tried to quiet the class, but it was impossible for me to have a louder voice than the yelling of forty boys and girls. Finally I had to give up, left the classroom and went back to my office sadly. The class was spoiled.
>
> But I was not the most unfortunate teacher in the school. Some of the teachers were hit by their students with bricks. The panes of their houses were broken. Sometimes a student's father or brother might come to school to help the boy to beat the teacher. In those chaotic years, a teacher did not have the right to speak as an ordinary person, sometimes could not even protect himself, to say nothing of helping his students to make progress. So the most important condition under which a teacher can give help to his students is a peaceful social environment.[1]

In 1979 China began a five-year plan for modernization. The plan included five priorities for development and change including the educational system's goals. In a speech to our group in the fall of 1985, Xu Fuji, the Director of the Bureau of Higher Education in Jiangsu Province, summed it up in this manner:

Chinese education had stressed rote learning and respect for authority. Xu said China must do away with the outmoded educational system. China needs to produce people who will think practically and independently, people who will have new ideas. China needs to promote creativity and inquisitiveness. China's modernization program includes a higher portion of the State budget for education,

---

1 The beginning of an essay by Zhu Yun-zhong, Dec. 2, 1985.

and China is trying to raise the status of the teaching profession.

During the school year 1985/86 we taught at a teacher's university where all of the students were studying to become teachers. A majority of our students, however, would have preferred some other profession. This was reflected in some of their essays:

> Once I heard that I would be studying here, at Teachers' University, I was a bit disappointed. My father was a teacher and now he still is. I know how the public looked on the teachers.[2]

> To be frank, teacher: the occupation itself is not to my will. My ambition instead, has always been an interpreter.

In an attempt to generate the traditional respect for teachers, the Chinese government implemented a National Teachers' Recognition Day to be celebrated each year in early September. On September 10, 1985, at the Nanjing Teachers' University, a very impressive program was presented. Since space was limited, only those teachers who had taught for twenty years were invited. My wife and I represented the foreign community. As we approached the Reception Building we were greeted by a Chinese colleague who escorted us inside. We were met by flood lights and television cameras. The cameras were focused on the guest book. As I stepped forward to sign my name, I could see the other "signatures", Chinese characters artistically written with Chinese writing brushes and black ink. I could not write my name with the writing brush; I had to use a pen. How plain my signature looked among all the others.

The speaker was Gu Xiu Lian, the governor of the province. She commended the university for its teacher graduates, but stressed the need for more teachers to support China's program to implement the current Chinese

---

[2] Excerpts from class writing assignments, Nanjing Normal University, 1985/86 .

goal of nine years of compulsory education. She said she had visited many elementary and secondary schools throughout the province and that they needed more teachers, better qualified teachers, and more help in general.

The needs that Governor Gu referred to were also mentioned in some of our student essays:

> I was born in 1965 in a small village. My family is a peasant one. . ..At that time, in a village, the school condition was very poor, no stools, no desks, no good classrooms. We had to take them ourselves. The level of the teachers was low too.[3]

Although most of our students would have preferred to do something other than teach, they were all very pleased to be studying at the university:

> It is a glory for me to be a second-year student at Nanjing Normal University.

A Clash in Cultures

In preparation for a class dealing with periodicals and newspapers I had subscribed to the airmail edition of *Time* magazine and two months of the *Sacramento Bee* newspaper before we left for China. I had also brought to China a dozen assorted magazines, including *Readers Digest, National Geographic, Better Homes and Gardens,* and *The Smithsonian.*

When I arrived in China I went to the office and asked the department chairperson, "Is there a course of study for the class?"

He said, "No, the class has never been taught before."

"What materials would you like me to use?"

---

[3] Excerpts from class writing assignments, Nanjing Normal University, 1985/86.

"You may use anything you want to." (That's Chinese for "We do not have any materials for the class.")

I was still unsure how to lay out the course. On Thursday morning at 10:30 I walked into the classroom. There were sixty-four students, about equally divided between men and women. They were all short, very slender, and they all had black hair and smiling faces. Some of the desks were made for three students, some for only two. They all sat on bench type seats that were fastened to the bare cement floor. The young men sat next to the young men; the young women sat next to the other young women. The cement walls were bare. There were spittoons in the hallways, but none inside the classrooms. That was to discourage students from spitting during class, but the lack of a spittoon did not seem to be a deterrent, although there were many public signs saying, "Do not spit." Spitting is one of those cultural things that foreign teachers have difficulty adjusting to. In the front of the room was a pitted chalk board with a wide chalk tray already filled with dust from the soft Chinese chalk. It was obvious the classroom had not been cleaned before this, the first day of class. There was a lectern on a raised cement platform in the front of the room. It is significant that classes in China are called "lectures." With sixty-four students, how would I conduct a classroom discussion on readings in a western periodical?

I began the class by asking the students, "What American magazines have you read, or better yet, what magazines have you ever seen, or had the opportunity to look through?" I was surprised by their answers: "None."

"None of the newspapers or magazines has been read."

"I've never seen any of those magazines."

"*Time*. I only looked at it. I knew nothing about it."

These were university juniors who were English majors and had studied English for eight years. Western magazines are simply not available in most areas in China, including universities where students are majoring in English and preparing to become English teachers.

I found that some of the students listened to Voice of America and the British Broadcasting Corporation on a regular basis and were well informed on international news, but most of the students did not and they were completely uninformed.

I selected several articles from my magazines and went to the department office to have copies made for my students. I was informed that there was only one copy machine on the entire campus, there were four thousand students, and that copies would be too expensive for me to request class sets. There was a department typist, however. I could submit articles to him and with a two week notice, he would type mimeograph stencils and prepare class sets for me. I had to proof read the mimeographed articles carefully because English was a second language for the typist also.

The library purchased a class set of *Time,* but they bought them two years old in order to get a better price. I found that teaching about world political events that were two years old was less sensitive to my students who lived in a communist setting and attended required political classes of their own twice a week. After I received the class set of current *Time* magazines from Hong Kong, however, the students were less interested in the two-year-old magazines.

I used *Time* magazine because it was available, but I found that it was very difficult for the students, partly because of the extensive vocabulary contained in the material, but also because of the political/cultural background expected of the reader. The university students in China (probably true for U.S. students as well) know so little about current events around the world. To help them better understand the world scene, I identified ten hot spots, for example, Nicaragua, the Middle East, Korea, Afghanistan, and gave them lectures on the historical, geographical, and political backgrounds of those areas. I never received any repercussions from any of my students or from anyone else regarding what was said in that class.

One day when the class was over, I went out into the hall and four or five of the male students were waiting for me. At first we talked in very general terms, but then they started asking very specific questions:

"Do you believe in letting a country settle its own problems?"

"Yes."

"Then why did your country invade Korea in 1950?"

I knew that I should avoid comprehensive political discussions, so I merely said, "Why did your country cross the Yalu River in 1951?" They said nothing further on that topic.

"Why did the United States follow a policy of isolationism after the first World War?"

Again I simply raised another question, "Why did China follow a policy of isolationism after "Liberation" in 1949?"

The young men made a habit of talking to me in the hall after class. They were never belligerent and they never pushed a point very far. On one occasion one of them said, "Our country disagrees with you on that point." I said, "I know it."

I tried to avoid public discussion of sensitive issues in class, and so did the students. It was during that fall semester that the United States bombed Libya. When one of my students asked, during class, "Why did the United States bomb Libya?" I gave him the latest copy of the *Time* magazine that covered that item and said, "Perhaps you would like to read this."

One day I assigned a writing assignment in class. The students worked very diligently until the bell rang and then most of them left. In the next five to ten minutes, all of the remaining students left except two. I became concerned that they were so conscientious on completing their assignment. When I went to their desks to see what was taking so long, I was surprised to see they were just looking at the ads.

Toward the end of the fall semester I began planning a final examination. When one teaches a content course in a class's second language, the factual data must remain simple. I prepared a three part examination. The first part was a map exercise requiring the identification of seventy-five nations. Part II was a vocabulary exercise requiring the students to write definitions. Both parts would be presented to the students in advance, and the students could memorize the answers.

Chinese students are accustomed to memorizing everything and are very skillful at it. I was not satisfied with a final examination that everyone would master perfectly. I prepared one more part: "On the exam I will give you five of the ten *hot spots*, and I will expect you to describe *briefly* the geography, the chief exports, the current political system and when and how that political system was established." Furthermore, in order to give you more time to complete the exam, I will give Part I the previous week and Parts II and III the final week.

When I described what would be expected on the final examination the class was very upset.

"We do not think you should give us that examination."

"The examination is unfair."

"You should just give us Parts I and II."

Chinese students are very grade conscious, but I intended to grade Part III very leniently, so I ignored their complaints. I passed out sample maps and gave them vocabulary lists to guide their study. When the class was over I talked with "my boys" out in the hall.

"Why are they so upset with the final?"

"I think some of them are afraid the final will be too difficult; they will not be able to memorize everything before the test. Others are upset because the format is different from what they are used to."

I decided to proceed as planned. The next week I gave Part I, the map identification, and over ninety percent of the students were able to identify all of the nations correctly.

The following week when I walked into the room, the class was all abuzz. When the bell rang, several students said,

"We should not have to take this test."

"This examination is unfair."

"Do not give us this test."

I explained to them that in class I had presented the geographical, historical, and political facts for each of the countries. I reminded them that I had written these on the board so they could copy them down. I encouraged them by stating I did not expect great detail. My arguments were to no avail.

When the students realized that I intended to give the examination as described, five or six of the class leaders came up to my desk. They were led by Han Xui Lian. She was taller than most of her classmates and more outspoken than the typical Chinese co-ed. Her voice could be heard on the public address system every morning at ten o'clock when a university sponsored English lesson was presented. The students reiterated their previous remarks, focusing on the exam being unfair.

Then Han Xui Lian said, "Do not give us this test. If you give us this test, many of us will not sign up for your class next semester."

In thirty years of teaching and administration in California I had never experienced a student protest like this. I was facing sixty-four students, all about twenty-one years old. I was in a foreign culture. Although their message was very clear, I could not predict their reactions. I decided to remain firm.

"My salary is not based on the number of students that I have enrolled in my class, so please sit down and let's start the final examination."

It was nip and tuck for awhile, whether they were going to go back to their seats and sit down. I did not wait; I began passing out the exams.

The students did very well on all three parts of the examination, but only twenty-seven students enrolled in the spring semester class, and Han Xui Lian was not one of them.

I was very satisfied with the smaller section in the spring semester because I was able to conduct class discussions on "readings in western periodicals and newspapers." But I recognized that I had had a real confrontation and have tried to analyze some of the elements in the situation. First, students in China apparently are used to considerable influence on class procedures. Second, the world knows how hard Chinese students study in elementary and middle school in order to pass the required entrance examinations for college or university. People are not so aware of how some of these same students slack off once they have the security of being a college student. We were not expected to fail any student. If any of our students did fail, we were asked to prepare a make-up examination so the student could try again. The university staff went to great lengths to help every student graduate.

Introduction to a Student Essay

Our students/teachers in Nanjing were all English majors and/or teaching English at the college level so their English skills, particularly their reading and writing skills were quite good. We learned a great deal about Chinese life and Chinese culture from reading their essays.

In one class of teachers I assigned the topic, "Discipline of young children in China." Here is a delightful story of Zhong Xi when she and her two brothers were disciplined by their mother, an ardent member of the Communist Party and a political official. When Zhong Xi was in my class she was twenty-nine years old and on sabbatical leave from her position as a teacher of English at the Forestry University in Nanjing. She had one child, a girl, who was staying with the grandmother in Shanghai until the girl reached three years old, the minimum age for the Nanjing University nursery school.

Student Essay—Our Childhood

There are three children in my family, my two brothers and I. We were born respectively in 1954, 1955, and 1956. Because of our close ages, we were able to play the same things together. And I cannot recall my childhood without mentioning them.

My mother was a political official. She was very conscientious and serious with her work, and of course, she had also a particular way to educate her children. In the year when we had finished our kindergarten and it was still too early for primary school, we were often locked indoors when my mother and father went to work because my mother did not allow us to play with other boys. Actually she regarded most of the kids around us were bad. After my parents had left, we would search the rooms for everything that might draw our attention or for us to play with in order to idle away the time. My mother had a cupboard in which she kept biscuits, candy, cakes, dried dates, etc. It was always locked of course, but one day, my elder brother happened to pull it hard and unlock it! Then he shared the things he took out with us for fear of our revealing the secret. After that, we locked the cupboard as usual. We did the same thing whenever we were left alone. Yet, the entertainment only lasted for one month or so until my mother found it out. Each of us suffered a good beating, and the useless small lock was changed into a new, big one.

My mother was very strict with us during our childhood. Her motto was that, dutiful sons came out of hard beatings. She had a club and a ruler as her equipment to punish us. None of us was not afraid of her then, like none of the rats was not afraid of cats.

One afternoon, we were again locked in the house. Suddenly I found the key had been left carelessly by my father on the bed. We were all excited to see that. We stood at the window, expecting some other children to pass by. Before long the door was opened by a kid with the key from the outside. We came out, as birds came out of the cage! We ran to the carpenter's workshop for we knew there was a see-saw there. Joyfully I played, first with my elder brother and then, the younger one. Upwards! Downwards! How happy we were! Just then, someone shouted, "Look! Your mother is coming!" What a thunder it seemed to us! I jumped down at once from my end and left my brother fall to the ground and he broke his arm! When Mother came and saw this, she was both angry and anxious. The result of this accident was that we two big ones got another severe punishment that evening, and the youngest one suffered as long as two weeks before his splints and bandage were taken off.

Generally speaking, we three children played very well, and cooperated very well too. But sometimes, we would betray one another, report each other's wrong doings and behaved like an apple-polisher. Once, my elder brother took several pieces of iron cakes from one of the factory workshops. He gave them to a peddler for some home-made candy. It was discovered by a worker who scolded my brother. Then, that evening, my younger brother told Mother all about it. She got angry at once and demanded the *criminal* to stand before her. She then asked me to pass her the club behind the door, but I did not. I was shivering all over then! My younger brother was quite willing to be the helper. It was not nice. I thought at that moment, I would never forget it!

My mother often taught us how to behave; asked us to always have good manners, to tell no lies, to keep our word and so on. One day we were having lunch around the table when my younger brother rushed in. He had been playing with other kids outside. When he saw all of us were eating, he came and joined us immediately without a word. My mother suddenly put down her chopsticks violently on the table, and remarked sternly to my younger brother, "Stop eating! Since you have no parents in your eyes, you should not eat the meal then!" All of us were silent, and I could even hear my heart beating! At last, my brother called, "Papa; Mama," before he was permitted to go on with his meal.

Besides all the family discipline for all three of us, there were still some more for me in particular. It was simply because I was a girl! The rules like, "You could not leave the table before you had finished your last mouthful of bread," "You could not sing or dance or kick anything while walking." "You could not stand reading or sit like a bow." "You could not go to other's houses at meal or bed time." "You could not play too much with boys," "You could not take or eat other's things," and "You could not even laugh too loud!"

When we began our primary school days, my mother changed much of her policies. She began to use mouth education more and hands less. Even so, whenever we were criticized by her we dared not talk back, and we must obey almost everything and anything she uttered. The most important change was that she began to ask us to write letters of guarantee when we had done anything wrong. She hammered three nails on the walls with three pegs hanging on the three nails which were respectively for us three children. Then she would peg the letters of guarantee whenever we wrote and hang them there on the wall like an exhibition. At the end of each month she would take them down, count them and see who wrote the most. Of course, the less you wrote, the better you were. Then, you would get a reward—two pencils, two notebooks or a film ticket.

I still think that my mother was a very strict mother. She sometimes was really too hard on us. Yet, many of our neighbors and her colleagues said that she was good at educating children, and followed her example. Now about two dozen years have passed. We three are all university or college graduates. My elder brother chose the subject of art, my younger brother physics, and I,

English. We are now working in different fields, yet, when we have time to meet together, we still recall our unforgettable childhood.

Zhong Xi
December 2, 1985.

Schools in China, including colleges and universities, hold classes six days a week, Monday through Saturday. Factories and businesses are also in operation six days a week. Although Sunday is the most popular day for factories and businesses to be closed, many of them are closed on some day other than Sunday. In the spring semester of 1986 I taught an evening adult class. My students were employed during the daytime and attended classes during the evening. Since they were no longer college-age, they gave a community perspective to their writing. For one of their assignments I asked them to describe how they spend their day off.

Student Essay—The Busiest Day in the Week

Sunday is usually the most leisurely day in the week. On this day people have much more leisure to do what they like and have a good rest. But for me, things are quite different. My Sunday falls on Saturday which is our factory's day off, while my husband and daughter have their rest day on Sunday. So I often have to spend my rest day alone, yet seldom do I feel lonely, because I am always fully occupied and as busy as a bee on that day.

On my rest day morning, I often get up a little bit earlier than usual and then rush into the food market, because occasionally I can buy something which is in short supply. On my way home from the market, I often buy some cakes and deep-fried twisted dough sticks for breakfast. (Usually in the morning we have no time to stand in a long queue to buy these things.) After breakfast, I begin to clean up the room, collect all the things which need washing and put them into the washing machine. Then I turn on the machine and the tape recorder at the same time. While the machine is working, I am busy preparing lunch and dinner, and listening to the tape on which I recorded some English programs and French lessons. As is often the case, I can't finish these few household chores until about eleven o'clock so I have to devote most of the morning to these things.

In the afternoon, sometimes I have even more things to do than in the morning. Being a teacher and a student, I must prepare lessons, correct exercise books for my students and also have to review and preview what I learned in the evening university and finish my homework, such as write out a composition assigned by Dr. Dameron. In addition to this, being a wife and a mother, I must go shopping, do some sewing or go to my daughter's school at times.

In the evening, I have classes in the evening university from 6:30 to 8:20. Immediately after I get home from the school, I turn on the radio and listen to the Voice of America for at least half an hour by habit. When I go to bed, I'm almost exhausted.

My Sunday is really the busiest day in the week.

Zheng Kai Di
Spring 1986

Leona taught seven sections of first and second year composition. Each class had thirty students and met once a week for two hours. Leona focused on communicating through writing. She presented sample paragraphs. She introduced her students to Journal Writing, that is, having each student write personal thoughts in his/her own journal for five or ten minutes each day without any correction of grammar or writing mechanics. She also had her students write on assigned topics that made them think: "My favorite room" provided many insights into Chinese family life, and "The animal I dislike the most" told us more about rats than we needed to know. The Chinese student writing was very graphic. The writings included many similes and descriptive words that would not be used in western writing, but which reflected a sensitivity to nature and interpersonal relationships. There is also great respect for the elderly, but I was a little shocked to find that someone aged sixty was considered to be an old man. The following essay was written by one of Leona's female students in a sophomore composition class.

Student Essay—The Perfect Picture

"There is only one left and it is the last one." I looked at my camera and looked round the surroundings while thinking what pictures I was going to take. I was going to send two or three photographs to be chosen for the Sixth Youth Photographic Exhibition, so I chose every scene seriously and took every picture carefully. It was dusk and I was standing on the bank of the river which seemed to be covered by thick and high reeds. The big summer sun in beautiful orange color was going down; bit by bit it came nearer to the water. All things were painted in the yellow-red clothes: the water flowing in the river, the tips of reeds and the hair and the dress of mine. Though it was still midsummer, it was not very hot in the dusk with a soft warm wind blowing from the surface of the river. I was just observing with great interest several wild ducks playing and swimming in the water, when I heard the voice of an old man, "Hello, girls!" I turned round and saw an old man about sixty sitting on a big stone; an old stick stood straight under his two hands. He was really old with all his hair turning white and grey. The wrinkles on his face gave me the impression that his life was full of unfortunate and bitter memory. But from his wrinkled small eyes I saw the kindness and affability as well as sorrow. I smiled to him and said hello to the old man. He stared at me for a moment and then nodded, "Ah, she wore that sun-red dress too. Several years ago, she was the same age as you." Who was she, I wondered? "Is she your daughter?" I asked. Suddenly a glimmer of a smile appeared on the corners of the old man's mouth. His face became bright and his eyes reflected the color of sunset. "She used to take care of me as if she were my own daughter." Then the old man seemed to begin recalling the past time. It was obvious that kind girl was now no longer a companion of the old man. I tried to guess what things happened to the girl and the old man and so to console him. But I thought I'd better not disturb the calmness and the nice memories.

The sun was half down the river and in the far distance the cloud was purple-red and the water was as scarlet as fire. The reeds were still waving in the evening breeze. Suddenly an idea flashed into my mind. Why not take a picture of the old man? That will be the best of all the pictures I had taken. Just at that moment I caught sight of two big teardrops welling up in the old man's eyes. He must be thinking of something bitter and sad. Quickly I made a decision and set up my tripod and turned the camera lens and focal distance correctly toward the old man. Then after I turned up the automatic shutter, I went to sit down close beside the old man. The old man woke up from his recollections. With the teardrops still on his face, the old man smiled at me with kindness and then released his right arm closing around my shoulders forcefully. I put my head against his chest, listening to his heartbeat and feeling his warm breast rising and falling. The air was quiet and we both heard the sound of the shutter, but neither of us moved.

Li Hong Mei
Spring 1986

We learned many things about China by reading our students' papers. We found that they were more willing to present opinions, attitudes, and personal feelings in an essay than in a face-to-face conversation. To capitalize on this fact and to develop a starting point for teaching American culture, I asked my students to list five things that are similar and five things that are different between their country and the United States. We Americans are always interested in how people from other countries view us. Here is a consolidation of the Chinese viewpoints of Americans from the periodicals class, sixty-four university juniors, including their generalizations and stereotypes.

Through the Chinese Looking Glass[4]

Most American people are outgoing, active, aggressive, talkative, and independent. They have a sense of humor. Americans like sports, and pay attention to nutrition and efficiency. American clothes are very modern and colorful and fit them well. Americans have a high rate of divorce and a high crime rate. They think money and individual freedom are important. The American people are peace-loving, but sometimes the U. S. government likes to wage wars against other countries with whatever excuses they can find.

America is a developed country with high living standards. Every family has television sets, recorders, refrigerators, etc. Americans have cars and they like to travel during holidays. They move frequently from one city to another.

The U.S.A. is a democratic country and is reputed to be a classless society, but the whole nation is controlled by a few millionaires. Trade and industry are organized and controlled by the capitalists. Workers are easily dismissed if the employer is not satisfied with them. Every year there are thousands of people out of work, including many university graduates. During an economic crisis, like the period of the Great Depression, workers suffer from hunger and poverty because they do not have jobs.

In America the relationship between people is not very good; people do not help each other. Also the crime rate is

---

4 *The Lodi News Sentinel*, April 11, 1986.

very high. Although Americans are rich in material things, they are poor in spiritual matters, especially young people.

There is no age limit for Americans to enter college. Students do not have to pass an entrance examination, but may attend any university they wish if they have enough money. College students are financially independent, getting their money from part time jobs. American college students can date, live with the opposite sex without getting married, or get married and even have children while they are still in college. American students are very active in class. They can interrupt their teachers and ask questions at any time. They can say anything they want to and are not afraid of making mistakes. American students can change their majors or even quit altogether and go back to school whenever they wish. But when students graduate, they may have difficulty finding a job.

Pornography is prevalent in the United States. It injures many young men and many crimes happen on account of it.

In the United States when children grow up, they want to be independent, so they move away from their parents. As their parents grow old, they become lonely and unhappy. When someone is too old to take care of himself, he must live in the old men's home. Even though he is looked after by nurses, he will be lonely and sad.

These impressions of America are based on the Chinese students' readings in classes, the weekly or bi-weekly political studies lectures which all university students are required to attend, and rather limited world news. China began to open its doors to the world in 1979, but there is considerable interpretation of any news coming from western countries.

Voice of America—A Chinese Experience

Since the Voice of America, or VOA as it is called, does not broadcast in the United States, few Americans are aware of the nature of the programing, or the effect VOA has in foreign countries. I was surprised by my students' responses when I asked them to write about the Voice of America from their perspective.

> I started listening to VOA in my last year in high school, about six years ago. Over the years I have been keeping in touch with VOA, and this has gradually made me a regular listener. At the very beginning, there was nothing but a few words here and there that I could recognize. This, for a long time, annoyed me, and I almost lost hope, Encouraged by my teacher, however, I cheered up and kept listening every day, skipping over all the new words and totally ignoring the complete meaning of each sentence. Day after day, week after week, month after month, a miracle appeared in me—one day when I was talking with several students in English, I suddenly found that I could think in English! Thanks to God, I have by no means wasted my efforts.

> Anyone who learns English here in China gets familiar with the British Broadcasting Company and the Voice of America. Some keen students have even made friends with either BBC or VOA, for they think they are of a great help to them in their acquisition of the English language. VOA in particular, I should like to mention here, is becoming more and more popular in China because of the wide and strong American influence on the one hand and the milder and more pleasant sound and intonations, one of the characteristics of the American English, on the other.

In China, Voice of America broadcasts programs from six o'clock a. m. to nine o'clock a. m. seven days a week. During this time there are programs of news, interviews, and special English summary of the weekly news. *Special English* is a simplified version of the news presented at a slower pace for the listeners who are learning English. Voice of America also broadcasts from six o'clock in the evening until midnight on week days. These programs include news, new music, country music, Jazz Hour, Magazine Show and Editorial.

> I have been listening to VOA for nearly three years. During the Cultural Revolution listening to VOA was illegal in China; it was regarded as one of the enemy's broadcasting stations by our government, so no one was allowed to listen to it. With the improvement of relationships between China and the U.S.A. our government began its open policy and to absorb more and more whatever is profitable to China from foreign countries, so now we are glad that we can listen to VOA and VOA has become a best friend for us.
>
> Now in universities, almost all foreign languages departments have opened listening courses as one of the student's major courses. These foreign languages departments record several programs of VOA and use them as English students' listening materials because the pronunciation and tone of VOA's announcers are very good and pleasant to listen to. When we listen to them, it is really an enjoyment. We are also surprised at how efficiently the news reporters work in the world. A thing happens somewhere in the world in the morning, and we hear the news reporter present it that afternoon.

Leona and I listened to the Voice of America to be able to respond to students' comments and questions concerning the top news stories of the day. We found that we were teaching more than just English.

Teaching Middle School Teachers

We arrived at the Jiangxi Teachers University on August 29, 1990. We had been assigned to the Training Center, a special department of the university, to develop a one year curriculum which would serve as a refresher course for middle school teachers of English. There were over thirteen thousand teachers of English in the middle schools of

Jiangxi Province, and, being a less developed province, over ninety percent had never graduated from college. In fact, most of them had had less than two years of college. We anticipated a class of forty teachers. We would divide the group in half for six hours of conversation each week. We would teach the total group in two-hour classes of reading, writing and the culture of western nations. Because the teachers were not college trained, I was also asked to teach methodology, or "how to teach English as a second language to classes of sixty junior and senior high school students."

On Monday morning twenty-four middle-school teachers walked into the classroom. Scared and homesick, they took their places. They had moved into the dormitories over the week-end. They had traveled by train for five to ten hours, or by a combination of train and bus for one or two days to get to the university. They were all married, except one. They had left homes and families to come to the university. Now they would live six to a room, eat university food, and try to learn English. They were aged twenty-six to forty-five and many of them felt they were too old to learn. They had been teaching English for five to fifteen years, but their English was so limited, they usually taught English in Chinese. They soon became very homesick for their families.

We interviewed them to determine their English level in order to assign them to the proper conversation class.

"How long have you been teaching English?"

"Are you married?"

"How many children do you have?"

"How old are they?"

The teachers were petrified. Many of them had never talked to a native English speaker before. If they could understand the questions we asked, we put them in the fast group.

The Training Center formed a supervisory committee for our program consisting of the Training Center Director, two of the Chinese teachers, the class monitor, and Leona and me. The class monitor was the oldest male student, aged forty-four. Since his English was very weak, we assumed he had been selected class monitor because of his age. The committee met about twice a month and discussed curriculum, text books, examination schedules, teaching effectiveness and any student problems. Our first meeting was held at the end of the first week. We met in our apartment. Leona served tea and I took the minutes. After the customary pleasantries, we discussed the first item of business. In China we found that people generally begin with minor, unimportant issues. The major problems are saved for the middle or even the end of the meeting. Whenever anything important was discussed, someone would translate it for the class monitor.

After discussing minor issues for about fifteen minutes, the Director said,

"The students are very depressed." "They cannot understand the instruction, the books are too difficult, and three of them have packed their bags and are ready to go home."

After considerable discussion the Chinese teachers and Leona and I agreed to change to easier books, schedule an additional two hour class for individual help, and that everyone would proceed more slowly in every class. We also agreed that the Director would remind the students that we expected them to work very hard, that this was a great opportunity for them and that they should take advantage of it. We did lose one student, but the other two unpacked their bags and we continued. It had been a long time since these teachers had been students and had been away from their homes, and the adjustment was difficult. They and their families also recognized how privileged they were to be studying under native speaking teachers at the university.

Although the writing of the middle school teachers was not as proficient in English as the college teacher/students had been in Nanjing in 1985/86, we found their essays very informative and entertaining also. I appreciated the insight into family life in this essay on National Day, the Chinese

Independence Day and the Mid Autumn Festival. The students were given a three-day vacation, and this student essay is a statement of anticipation.

National Day Holidays With My Family

National Day is approaching. I'm going to be with my family, but I don't want to go anywhere. After leaving home for a month, something must be very dirty in my house. So I have to stay at home and do some cleaning—washing quilts, cleaning the furniture and sweeping the floor.

On October 3 we'll also have Mid Autumn Festival. I'll invite my father to have dinner with us because he has no sons, but a daughter. I'll give him some presents—two boxes of moon cakes, two bottles of wine, and some apples.

In the morning my husband will go to the street to do some shopping for the big meals. We'll have some pork, fish, chicken, sausage, vegetables, beer and moon cakes. After lunch my daughter of fifteen will sing us a song about the moon. It will be very nice.

Traditionally, we'll take a basin of water outside in the evening, so that we can see how beautiful the moon's reflection is. There will be all kinds of colors—red, orange, yellow, green, black, blue and purple. That will be very funny.

I think we'll have a good time during the holidays.

Liu Ai Mei
September 1990

Part of our charge in China was to teach our students methodology. We had seen the enthusiasm of the Chinese seventh graders begin to wane in the latter years of high school. Eleventh and twelfth graders became bored; they saw little practicality for Chinese students to learn English. We told our middle school teachers that they must make the teaching of English more interesting and to do that, it must become more relevant. Involve students in the learning process and change their language practice from textbook drills to real communication. We did conduct the usual dialogue drills, and our students loved the Total Physical Response activities. Total Physical Response or TPR is a method in which the learner utilizes a physical response, e. g. stands up, points, touches, in order to enhance the audio and lingual paths of learning. We also used drama, role playing, games, songs, and a model store. To go beyond this, however, we tried other activities.

To provide an opportunity to practice public speaking in the advanced conversation class, Leona told her students to assume that the university was a city and that it was run by a city council. She then asked her better students to prepare campaign speeches that would include the things they could do to improve the campus if they were elected, and she asked other students to prepare nomination speeches to nominate those who were running. She then took the class on a walking tour of the campus to look for things that needed to be improved. After the speeches were delivered, the class held an election. The top two candidates and their campaign managers then presented their speeches to my American culture class.

Toni Presents a Nomination Speech

(We gave them English names at their request.)

I'm very glad to introduce Lucy to you. She is a candidate for city council. I'm very glad to nominate Lucy to run for our city council of Jiangxi Normal University. Lucy is still very young. She is also a very ambitious woman. After she graduated from Beijing Qin Hua University she devoted herself to educational cause.

She has taught for about fourteen years. She is not only strict with herself, but also in her work. She is a good and experienced teacher. She speaks English very well. For several years she joined the Party and became a Party member. She always thinks of others and seldom thinks of herself. She is always ready to help others. She sets a good example for us. She was elected as an excellent Party member many times. If she wins the election, she will do a lot of things for us and our school. She will be able to win.

Lucy's Campaign Speech

It's lucky for me to have an opportunity to run for the city council here. I'm a loyal friend of yours, and I hope I can be a council member of this university and work for you. Maybe you will ask me, "What qualifications do you have to run for the council? And how can you improve the campus when you are elected?"

O. K. I'll say something about them. You see, I'm a Party member. This is the most important qualification to run a school today. And I've accepted a higher education. I've been a leader of the English teaching and research group for more than eight years, and accumulated a wealth of experience in leadership and organizations. I'm intelligent, unselfish and diligent—devoted to work, and also very honest and willing to accept good advice. I can get on well with people. So I think I've got enough qualifications to run for this campus.

If I am elected to the city council, I'll do six actual things to improve the school:

The first thing is to ask some famous architects to put up several new apartments for the teachers and try to increase their salary, so that they'll be proud of being a teacher and work hard for the Party and people.

> The Second: I'll have this building rebuilt. It is old, and dark and when spring comes, it gets quite damp. It's bad for our health and eyesight. I'll make it spacious, bright and modern, so that we can stay in a happy frame of mind, study and master more knowledge of foreign languages for going abroad.
>
> The Third: I'll make the School Library larger and more attractive, keeping more science books, storybooks, reference books, history books and magazines, so that all the teachers and students will have chances to choose what they want to read or borrow.
>
> The Fourth: I'll install air conditioners in each of the rooms in the basement to help the students study better in a cozy place in their spare time.
>
> The Fifth: I'll rebuild the sports ground. It is a bit small, and when it rains, it's full of mud. I'll turn it smooth and strong, so that the teachers and students can often have sports and other activities on it.
>
> The Sixth: The school hospital must be improved the working conditions, and add some equipment for the bad patients. Meanwhile I'll strengthen the management and improve the doctor's quality, so that they will serve the people heart and soul, and make the people in the whole campus responsive and full of love.
>
> With my help, I believe that our campus will become more beautiful, more lovely, and more modern! I will do some volunteer jobs for you. Thank you all.

One can learn about a people's priorities by listening to what is promised in a campaign speech. Notice what things the candidates promise to provide and what changes they would make in management practices. I will include the other candidate's campaign promises, but I will edit them for clarity and brevity.

Franklin's Campaign Speech

Ladies and Gentlemen:

I'm going to run for the council of this city. If I win this election, I'll change the features of this area, and make the lives of our people better and better.

1. I'll change the form of the administration at present, and change the incorrect styles of work. If you are lazy, you can't get much food for you and your family.

2. Put democracy into practice thoroughly and every council person can propose all of his opinions. We can gather all of them and make correct choices to construct our city.

3. As we know, the teachers' income is lower and only raise themselves. If they want to buy something a little more expensive such as a color TV, electric refrigerator, washing machine, etc. they have to tighten their belts. I think that what they devote is more than what they get. Up to now they have had bad conditions, and I want to give a special fund to increase teachers and build a lot of apartments for them.

4. I'll guarantee all kinds of supplies, such as fuel, water, electricity, food, coal and so on.

5. I'll improve the traffic conditions. It's very crowded in the street at rush-hour every day. We'll build several elevated bridges to change this condition. We must strengthen the management at the roads and prevent the accidents taking place everywhere. We must propagate the rules of traffic to make the people drive and walk in the street safely.

6. I'll get additional equipment for the hospital to keep the people in good health to work.

7. I'll provide places for entertainment. I'll set several clubs in the city so that the people can have a good time after their work.

8. I'll make the city green and plant many trees so the people can breathe fresh air.

9. The public order is the important thing to insure that the people have a good work condition and work safety.

10. I'll protect the human rights not to be attacked and everyone can speak what he wants freely, but all these must be in the limits of our country's law.

Which one would you vote for? In the class election Franklin won. Lucy told us later that she had voted for Franklin. Franklin won by one vote.

The Joys of Teaching—in China

Leona had ten students in her Conversation Class, five men and five women. The students were aged twenty-five to forty-five years old and all had been teaching English at the equivalent level to junior high school for many years.

In preparation for the mid-term, in which the students would be expected to present oral dialogues, Leona asked her students to pair-off. "Choose your own partner." Four pairs—two men, two men, two women, two women, were quickly formed. The odd woman just sat there. Leona quietly asked her if she would be willing to work with Mr. Wu.

"No!"

Mr. Wu was not very attractive, but these students are all married. Being careful not to force the issue, Leona had the other pairs practice quietly and then give their brief presentations. It was time for the break. Leona called Mrs. Qu to the back of the room and invited Mrs. Wang, a cadre, (leaders at various levels in China are referred to as a cadre,) to join them to see what could be done. Mrs. Qu had her head down on her desk and was on the verge of tears.

Leona leaned over her and quietly asked again, "Can you work with Mr. Wu?"

"No!"

Leona then asked Mrs. Wang, the cadre, "Then what shall we do?"

When no solution was forthcoming, Leona asked if they thought it would be acceptable if they re-arranged all of the pairs and made every group a man/woman pair. They thought that would be satisfactory.

Leona then put the five men's names in a box, and the five women's names in a different box. She went next door to get another teacher so she would have someone that was impartial to draw out the pairs. When the process was completed, everyone accepted the results. The teacher from next door returned to his class.

Leona asked the new groups to get together and practice for Monday's mid-term. All the new pairs got together, and began practicing, but no one would sit together. They practiced while standing up.

I think those teacher-students had been in junior high school too long.

Certified

Toward the end of the class break several students came back into the room. They were talking loudly in Chinese and waving their hands in the air. One student had a Chinese newspaper. It seemed to be the focus of the problem. She threw it down on her desk and four or five others all crowded around so they could get a better view. They all continued to talk. It sounded like a swarm of bees, only louder. Leona couldn't figure out what was wrong.

"What's the problem? Why is everyone so excited?"

One student started to explain and then said, "I cannot say it in English."

Other students came in, but many did not. Leona began the second half of the two-hour class without them.

Xiao Gan, an administrative assistant, came into the classroom to start the conversation exercise video tape.

"Xiao Gan, Why are the students so excited?"

"They aren't excited!"

"You can be excited and happy, or you can be excited and sad."

Xiao Gan just shrugged and left the room.

Without knowing about the previous events, I entered my classroom and began writing on the chalkboard. Xiao Gan came in.

"I think you should know what is happening, but if Director Xu talks to you, I haven't told you anything!" Xiao Gan then proceeded to explain, "As you know, the middle school teachers are enrolled in a Certificate Program. When the Training Center developed this program, we included the specific courses and the minimum number of hours required by the Province for the certificate. When our students complete the entire year, they will be issued certificates by the Province. Today in the *People's Daily* there is an article that states, 'Those persons receiving the educational certificate will not be automatically promoted nor will they automatically receive an increase in their salary.' The students feel they have been deceived. They think that if the certificate has no value, this year of study has no value, and they all want to go home. They are considering going home **today** and not staying to take their final examinations. Remember, I have not told you anything."

Most of the students came to my Extensive Reading Class that day, but no one talked to me about their problem. The class was over at noon, and Leona and I had no classes the rest of the day.

That evening, after dinner, Director Xu and an interpreter came to our apartment. We knew it was something important because he had brought the head of the Foreign Languages Department to serve as his interpreter.

"I suppose you have already heard about the students' problem."

"Oh, no, the students have not told us anything."

"There was an article in the paper today stating that the teachers' certificate will not guarantee an automatic promotion. The middle school teachers are very disappointed and they are all talking about going home and not staying for the final examinations."

I asked a question that any American would ask, but when I said it I realized how foreign my question was in their setting, "Does the statement in the newspaper reflect the official government position?" I mean, "Can we go on what the paper has said?"

Director Xu immediately softened his tone, "We are checking it out."

I then realized that in China no one questions what is in the paper because the paper **is** the government voice.

We discussed the situation at some length. Final examinations were only ten days away, and if the students left now they would have nothing.

Finally I said, "Even though the certificate will not guarantee instant promotion, I would assume that if a chance for promotion arises, the certificate would certainly be considered as one of the criteria for promotion."

Director Xu readily agreed.

"Then what we must do is to talk to the students and try to persuade them to stay at least and complete the finals, and then strongly encourage them to return for the spring semester and complete the certificate program as well."

Director Xu was very pleased at my response. He seemed surprised that we were so willing to help encourage the students to stay. This is apparently a cultural thing. They are reluctant to discuss their problems with a foreigner and then surprised at our support. Did he think we would laugh at their problem, or was it a question of "dirty laundry?" On our part, we were committed to the program and would certainly work hard to make it succeed.

The next morning the students attended Mr. Xie's Listening Class. He soon found that they didn't want to listen, they wanted to talk about their problem. Mr. Xie said later that he spent the entire two hours talking with them about their options.

Mr. Xie was pretty firm. He encouraged them to stay and take their finals, but he also reminded them that if they went home and then later changed their minds and wanted to come back, they should not expect him to give them late make-up exams!

I did not talk with the entire class, but whenever I had the chance, I talked with individuals and with small groups. I told them they were teachers. I said the reason they were there was to learn more English so they could do a better job of teaching. I reminded them that they would be English teachers the rest of their lives and that this opportunity may never be repeated for them.

I went to Director Xu and suggested he get a spokesperson from the provincial government to meet with the middle school teachers to explain to them what the official position was. Director Xu accepted the suggestion and someone from the government did come and talk with them.

After that meeting I asked, "Well, were the students convinced?"

"Not completely, but they haven't left yet."

As the days passed more and more of the students decided to stay, first for the final examinations, and gradually for the second semester as well. The crisis had passed.

Leona and I talked about the significance of this issue at great length and came up with two thoughts: first, it appears that personal reward and recognition are important in China also, and second, these teachers had been happy in their jobs and satisfied with their government. Now they had been promised something and then became disillusioned. We wondered if they would better understand the students at Tiananmen Square.[5]

[5] Students protested in Tiananmen Square in Beijing in April and May of 1989. On June 4th, 1989 the government suppressed the demonstrations with military force.

Chapter IV

Let's Go

At Nanjing Normal University in 1985/86 I taught a class of college teachers who were on sabbatical leave from their English teaching jobs in two and three year colleges from other parts of the province. During the year two of these teachers contacted the officials in their cities Nantong and Yanchen and arranged for our taking three-day lecture tours to their colleges. We were overwhelmed by the gracious reception we received by the colleges and by the city officials in each of these cities. In Nantong I was so impressed I asked our host, "Haven't you had any foreign visitors in your city?" He responded, "Oh yes, we had a woman from the World Health Organization of the United Nations about six months ago."

Nantong, the city we visited in December, is a very small city about fifty miles north of Shanghai, but the easiest way to get there from Nanjing was by boat.

The following article describing this boat trip to Nantong and the resultant lecture tour is based on an article published in *The Galt Herald* in January 1986.

Western Teachers Welcomed in Newly Opened City

The boat whistle sounded long and deep, impatient to start the two hundred mile trip down the Yangtze River to

Nantong. It was four fifteen on a warm December afternoon, and we had momentarily stepped back into our role as tourists, camera on one shoulder, and standing next to Samsonite luggage still showing that new look. As foreign guests we were a contrast to the crowded line of Chinese passengers with their burlap and cloth-wrapped bundles waiting to board. Foreign guests are given special treatment. We bypassed the line and were directed by our two Chinese companions to our quarters on the second deck. We were assigned a private cabin about eight feet by nine feet with two single beds, a wash basin, and a writing desk. There were only three other similar cabins on the boat. The cabins led to a private lounge in the bow, reserved for the special guests. Our two Chinese companions were assigned to a room with five sets of metal double bunks. There were a few pegs on the walls to hang things and one small table. The ten-person rooms were 'co-ed'. There were about six hundred passengers on board, many more passengers than the various rooms would accommodate. Dozens were sleeping on the deck and in all of the corridors throughout the ship.

As the boat swung out into the mile-wide river we went under the Nanjing Bridge, the pride of China. It was originally designed by Russian engineers, but when the Chinese government leaders asked all the Russians to leave in 1960, they took their bridge plans with them. The Chinese engineers then redesigned the bridge and built it themselves. Large boats, small boats, boats of traditional design, and tug boats pulling their strings of barges shared the channel. Some of the boats served as family residences. On one such boat, I saw a young woman washing her long black hair in an enamel wash basin. On another several young boys waved to us while chickens walked freely in and out of their cabin.

It was time for supper. Our two companions, who were escorting us to Nantong, led us to the ship's common dining room, located in the stern. The dining room would accommodate about two-hundred people at one time. The aroma of Chinese food filled the room. We sat on small backless stools at round wooden tables. The bare wooden tables contained only one item, a cup holding about fifty wooden chop sticks. One of our hosts selected two chop sticks. He took a small note book from his pocket, tore out a page, and then used the paper to wipe off the chop sticks. When he felt sure they were clean, he handed them to me; he repeated the process for Leona. Soon a waiter appeared, accepted the order, and brought several steaming bowls to the table. We ate rice, fish, and cabbage, using the recently sanitized chop sticks and eating directly from the common serving dishes. The food was tasty, and satisfying. We retired early because we would arrive in Nantong at two o'clock in the morning. At one o'clock in the morning there was a knock on our door. Groggily I stumbled to the door and opened it. A woman in a white uniform wanted to see our tickets. I presented them for her inspection and she left. I went back to bed. At one thirty a. m. I dreamily heard knocking at the door again. The same woman was there. She talked rapidly in Chinese and I did not understand her, but then she held up two fingers, and then five fingers. I thanked her, closed the door, and told Leona, "I assume we will arrive in Nantong at 2:05."

The boat was on schedule. Two more representatives from Nantong Teachers College, a three year college preparing teachers for secondary schools, were waiting with a van, and took us to a hotel. One of the hosts was the department chairperson, Zuo Biao, of the foreign languages department. On the way to the hotel he presented the following request.

"We are in luck! This weekend there is a group of one hundred librarians from colleges and universities all over China holding a conference at our college. Would you be so kind as to give them a lecture?"

It was two-thirty in the morning. I was riding in a van with gracious hosts, anticipating an exciting three days. What else could I say, but, "I would be happy to."

The next morning we were still getting dressed when we heard the knock at the hotel room door. I opened it, but was not prepared for the delegation that was standing there—the foreign affairs officer for the city, the vice-president of the university, the department chairperson, the foreign affairs officer for the college and an English teacher who was my student. We quickly finished dressing, fumbling with our buttons, knowing the delegation was now waiting out in the hall.

We all rode together in the school van. On the way to the college the department chairperson turned to me and asked, "What will you say to the librarians tomorrow?" It was at two-thirty that morning that he had originally asked me. I had to say, "I don't know yet."

As we drove into the parking lot at the college we were greeted by a large painted sign, *Warmly Welcome to our Institute.* We felt greatly honored.

Since this was a teachers' college, that afternoon I lectured on "Education in California." The audience included two hundred forty college students majoring in English and another one hundred fifty teachers of English from several colleges throughout the city. The lecture hall was a flat floor auditorium/cafeteria with a raised stage and a public address system. China's modernization includes the reform of education, the extension to nine years of compulsory education throughout China, and a change from the lecture-rote memory method to methods that will develop problem solvers and inquisitive minds. I, therefore, described a learner-centered approach and presented techniques for teaching analytical reading, critical writing, and the importance of research. I wondered how this would be received in a communist political setting. That evening we presented a collection of personal slides on California life and scenery to one hundred fifty students.

The following morning we met with two English classes for two periods, exchanging groups for the second hour, and conducted "free talk" with sophomores eager to learn more about the United States. Nantong had been open to foreign visitors for only two years and the college had never had a foreign teacher. A television crew came into the room, flood lights were turned on, and the camera began to roll. That night we watched ourselves on the evening news.

The students' excitement, reflected by their many questions, was portrayed by an elaborate colored chalk drawing on the black board saying "Welcome to the Damerons." Since we were the first western people these students had ever met, the students asked questions about our family, respect for teachers in American society, the life of the teenager, the generation gap, the equality of blacks and Native Americans, and whether Chinese students are clever. They also asked about the Geneva arms talks that were in progress at that time and the danger of AIDS.

Following the classes, the department chairperson again asked, "What will you tell the librarians?" I finally realized that the department chairperson would be translating my speech to the librarians, and he wanted the speech in advance to be better prepared. In China a lecture is one and one half hours long. Since the speech would be translated sentence by sentence as it was delivered, I needed a speech forty-five minutes long. Using hotel stationery, a rarity in Chinese hotels, I started writing.

That afternoon Leona lectured to four hundred students on pre-school and primary education stressing developing self concept and inquisitive minds through manipulating materials and making choices. At the same time I presented my lecture through an interpreter to one hundred librarians from fifty-six colleges and universities all over China. I described the role of the library as a tool for inquiry and research in American education. That evening we were feted at a banquet in a private home, the home of my student who had arranged for the lecture-tour. The Department Chairperson and the Foreign Affairs Officer attended also.

My student, Chen Ke Ping, and her husband had prepared a sixteen dish dinner. There were two different whole fish dishes, shrimp, jelly fish, sea cucumber, pork tendon (from the feet of the pig,) and a seaweed/coral growth called pine tree which grows on the bottom of the sea. The sea cucumber was cut in long slices that were so slippery I had trouble picking them up with chopsticks. All of these dishes were mixed with bamboo shoots, bean curd, mushrooms, Chinese cabbage, etc. The dinner was topped off with sweet rice soup, and finally a bowl of rice, and then an orange.

Chen Ke Ping's husband was twenty-nine years old and was a journalist. I asked him if he would write an article for me on Middle School Education in China. At first he agreed, but later sent his regrets through his wife. She explained that since he was a professional writer his boss would have to review it, and would ask why he was writing something for me, and he did not want to go through with that. If his wife would write it, there would be no problem. I was not surprised when he said no, but I was surprised at receiving an explanation. In China it is usually difficult to find out "Why?"

The following day there was sight seeing; a Buddhist temple, the Yangtze River (fourteen miles wide at this point), and a drive through the countryside. We went shopping for cotton print, a specialty in this textile town. Even the shopping was an experience. Any foreigner would be a curiosity, but our image was accentuated by our entourage—the foreign affairs officer, the vice-president of the university, the department chairperson, seven people in all. Our group became a magnet, attracting local onlookers, who crowded around us and made our show an even greater attraction.

That afternoon I lectured on California junior high and high school curriculum, student life, and student activities because students graduating from two and three year teachers colleges will teach at that level (they call it middle school.)

The college president hosted a farewell banquet that evening. There were many dishes and the Foreign Affairs Officer kept my plate full. The department chairperson was doing the same for Leona. We had three glasses, a large one for Chinese orange soda (at room temperature,) a middle sized glass for Chinese rice wine, and a small glass for whisky that looked like water. They do not serve tea at banquets.

While we were at the banquet table, someone came in and explained to our host that the librarians were having their banquet in the adjoining room and would Dr. and Mrs. Dameron come in and greet them. We walked into a room full of smiles and loud applause. I carried my glass of orange soda with me so I could present them with a toast. They were very responsive. It was a heady experience.

We had been overwhelmed by the gracious reception provided by the college staff. The sincerity of the college leadership was demonstrated by seven college and city officials, including the college president, going with us to the Port at nine-thirty that evening and staying with us in the van when the boat was late. Sitting there in the dark van we began singing, and we sang for almost three hours. The Chinese knew "Edel Weiss," "Doe Is a Deer, a Female Deer," and "Five Hundred Miles." Then we sang some additional American songs and they sang several traditional Chinese songs including the mimicking of Beijing opera. We had many laughs and a lot of fun. At one o'clock in the morning, the college president left, and we were taken to a hotel for Chinese. After only one hour, however, we were awakened, and boarded the boat for the twelve hour return trip upstream to Nanjing.

During the three day absence from Nanjing the weather changed from a warm December afternoon to twenty degree Fahrenheit temperature and a cold wind. Ponds were frozen and there was a light snowfall. The cold, however, could not erase the warm memories of enthusiastic students excited over firsthand impressions of America or college teachers searching for technical answers to grammatical phrases of the English language and new and more effective methods of teaching. We would never forget the interest, attention, and concern that had been attention, and concern that had been extended to us by our many hosts at the Nantong Teachers College.

Spring Trip to Yanchen

It was mid-April when we went on our next three-day lecture tour. The car from Yanchen arrived Wednesday noon. It was similar to a Ford Pinto, but it was a foreign model. There are very few American automobiles in China. We were accompanied by two English teachers from the three year Yanchen Educational College and the driver. After driving for about two hours we reached Yangzhou and then turned onto the levee road along the Grand Canal. The road was two-laned without a white line, and on each side there was a single row of trees spaced five to ten feet apart. The road reminded me of the levee road along the Sacramento River in California. There was some truck and bus traffic, enough bicycle traffic to be a nuisance, and occasional pedestrians.

The Grand Canal was old, picturesque, and busy. It was about one hundred twenty yards wide and carried numerous boats of various descriptions. Some went singly; some were linked together in long trains. The wind pushed the smaller boats with square sails, and diesel engines chug-chugged the heavier boats up and down the canal a chug at a time. The most common diesel boat was about forty feet long with a small square cabin providing living space in the stern. The forward two-thirds of the boat provided open cargo space. We turned onto river roads and lesser canal roads, and as we progressed we saw more of the smaller boats: some propelled by a large single oar, occasionally double oars, and sometimes being propelled by poling with a long bamboo pole. We also saw men walking the tow path, with a rope over their shoulder, pulling boats along the water course.

Again these roads were two-laned and tree-lined, and now with wheat fields beyond the trees. The wheat was planted in beds six to twelve feet wide, separated by small irrigation furrows. Small crop areas indicated farming by hand labor. The wheat was fifteen inches high and would be hand harvested in late May or June, and then rice would be planted. The smaller levee roads were filled with two-wheeled walking tractors pulling trailers of farm produce to market and many more bicycles. A hundred pound pink pig, similar to a Yorkshire, was lying crosswise on the back of a bicycle; one could say it was hog-tied. Domesticated white and brown ducks swam in the edges of the water-ways, tended by young boys with long flexible poles. There were frequent clusters of houses, mostly with red tile roofs, but some had thatched roofs, and the walls were generally made of brick. The better houses had red bricks, the poorer houses and the out-buildings were made of adobe bricks.

As we drove through many small villages, I never tired of the sights. We saw two or three pool tables outside along the main street with groups of young men playing or watching the play. Every village had swarms of people, farmers markets with fresh produce, thousands of two-wheeled carts and bicycles, and hundreds of two-wheeled walking tractors. We attracted attention as we drove through each village.

We arrived in Yanchen about six-thirty and went straight to the hotel. There was no heat in the hotel, and the hot water was turned on only at night from six to nine p. m. Since we gave lectures every night, we did not benefit from the hot water until the fourth night. Back in Nanjing we didn't have much heat or hot water so this lack was of no great significance. Other than that, the hotel was quite nice. We had been told to come down to the lobby at seven o'clock for an informal reception.

About ten minutes before seven o'clock we started getting ready. I had just changed into my suit and there was a knock at the door. It was five minutes before seven. I opened the door and there stood the president of the college, the dean of the English department, the foreign affairs officer, and two or three dignitaries including a lady who was in charge of all education for the entire city plus eight surrounding counties, representing a population of seven million people. Leona was not quite ready. I had to leave them standing in the hall, tell Leona the situation, and then go out and make small talk until Leona was ready. We had dinner in the hotel dining room. It was not very formal, except for all the toasts to everyone's health. There were many dishes, fifteen or twenty, and the food was very good. In typical Chinese fashion, when the leaders are finished eating, they excuse themselves, and the dinner is over. Chinese do not linger at the table afterwards.

At seven o'clock the next morning there was a knock at the door. This time it was only our two English teachers who then accompanied us to breakfast.

When we arrived at the college we were taken to the reception lounge and met the president, two deans, and several teachers. We were served sweets and a cup of tea. I was scheduled to give a lecture in a few minutes, but no one seemed to be concerned about the time. I like to go to a lecture hall a few minutes early and get ready. In China no one ever tells you in advance what to expect. You get used to waiting until someone else decides.

The president said it was time to go to the auditorium. Six college dignitaries escorted us to the large assembly hall/cafeteria. We entered through the rear door. The student body and the staff were already there; every seat was filled. As we entered the room, everyone stood and clapped, and they continued clapping as we walked the entire length of the aisle up to the front and onto the raised stage. The reception caused a tremendous feeling, a mixture of walking on air as we walked up the aisle, and a sense of anxiety as to whether we could fulfill their expectations once we got there.

The lengthy introductions were presented in Chinese since this audience included all of the teachers and staff, not just the English majors. We responded with a brief greeting that was translated. Then we were escorted back to the reception room and as we exited, everyone stood and clapped as they had done when we entered.

While we were drinking more tea, the English majors and staff moved to a smaller auditorium. We went to the auditorium and again they all stood and clapped as we came in. After a formal introduction I presented a lecture on teaching methodology. I began with a story: A school had a track team. They wanted the team to do well so they employed a great runner to coach their team. He *told* them how to run; since he was a great athlete he also *showed* them how to run, and being very conscientious, did this diligently every day, *but the team never ran.*

On the day of the race he said, "I have taught you everything I know about running; go out there and *win!*" Then I presented a parallel. There was a school which had an English class. They wanted a good class so they hired a great writer. He *told* them how to write, he *showed* them on the chalkboard. . . .But they *never did any writing.* I stressed, to teach writing, students must write, to teach speaking in a second language, students must speak, etc. I talked to a group of two-hundred students, all English majors. My lecture was two hours long. Following the lecture, the students submitted questions in writing. The question time was interrupted; the college president was ready to show me the campus.

Before going to Yanchen we were asked what we wanted to see. Among the alternatives offered was a tractor factory. I was raised on a farm and even now own a small Japanese made Kubota tractor. It had been an easy choice. Now I was having second thoughts. The tour was becoming so complicated.

We were accompanied by the college president, the dean of our department, the foreign affairs officer, several teachers, and a photographer who took pictures of us constantly. We were then greeted by the factory manager and several other factory leaders. We were taken to a reception room for tea. The factory manager sat next to me and through an interpreter told me about his factory. He said they make twenty thousand walking tractors a year. He said they make one thousand four wheeled tractors each year. He told me how many employees he had, and he described next year's production quotas. He was very proud of his plant. I listened attentively. I was interested, but it is difficult to carry on a meaningful conversation through an interpreter. Then I remembered, I had brought a picture of my Kubota. To teach culture we had brought pictures of home, and family, and daily life. My picture showed me riding in my Kubota and holding my year old granddaughter on my lap. The factory manager examined the picture for a long time, then smiled warmly, and asked, "May I keep it?" Now that I am back in the United States, sometimes I wonder, "Where is that picture now?"

After the tractor factory tour we visited a middle school. Every tour begins in the reception room where visitors are served tea and statistics. The school leaders were gracious hosts, and following the required preliminaries, the middle school English teachers all wanted their pictures taken with the foreigners who speak English. The campus was lovely. The library building was surrounded by water on three sides. There was attractive landscaping and a decorative fountain. The book collection, however, was limited. The books were printed on poor quality paper with few pictures and most of the volumes had paper covers. Because of the scarcity, and limited funds for acquisitions, librarians consider their primary role is to protect the books, rather than distribute them.

We also visited a general classroom with sixty boys and girls and then a computer class with thirty students and fifteen computers. The computer teacher was very personable, and the students were enthusiastic as they worked in teams of two on computers called Laser, a tape drive model made in China.

That evening we went back to the college, with our escorts, of course. I had developed a slide show on the United States, based on several trips across the country. We had also brought a video on teaching English as a Second

Leona and Ron with new bicycles in the courtyard of the Foreigners Guest House. Note study/living room windows.

Free Market Vendors in Beijing.

A pull cart loaded with wrecked and damaged bicycles in Nanchang.

Leona baking an apple pie in our bathroom. A frying pan with the handle removed served as a pie pan.

A pedi-tricycle being unloaded at the Friendship Store in Nanchang.

A pull cart loaded with barrels in Nanjing.

A Middle School Class (8th Grade) in Wangli, a suburb of Nanchang.

Leona's second year composition class in Nanjing Teacher's

Ron's Readings in Periodicals and Newspapers Class in Nanjing Teacher's University.

At the graduation banquet our Middle School Teacher Students toast us with warm beer in rice bowls. Lucy (see Ch. 3) is on the right.

The Training Center classroom was in the high forties, Fahrenheit, during the wintertime. We all wore many layers.

Leona plays ball at Kindergarten in Yanchen while dignitaries look on.

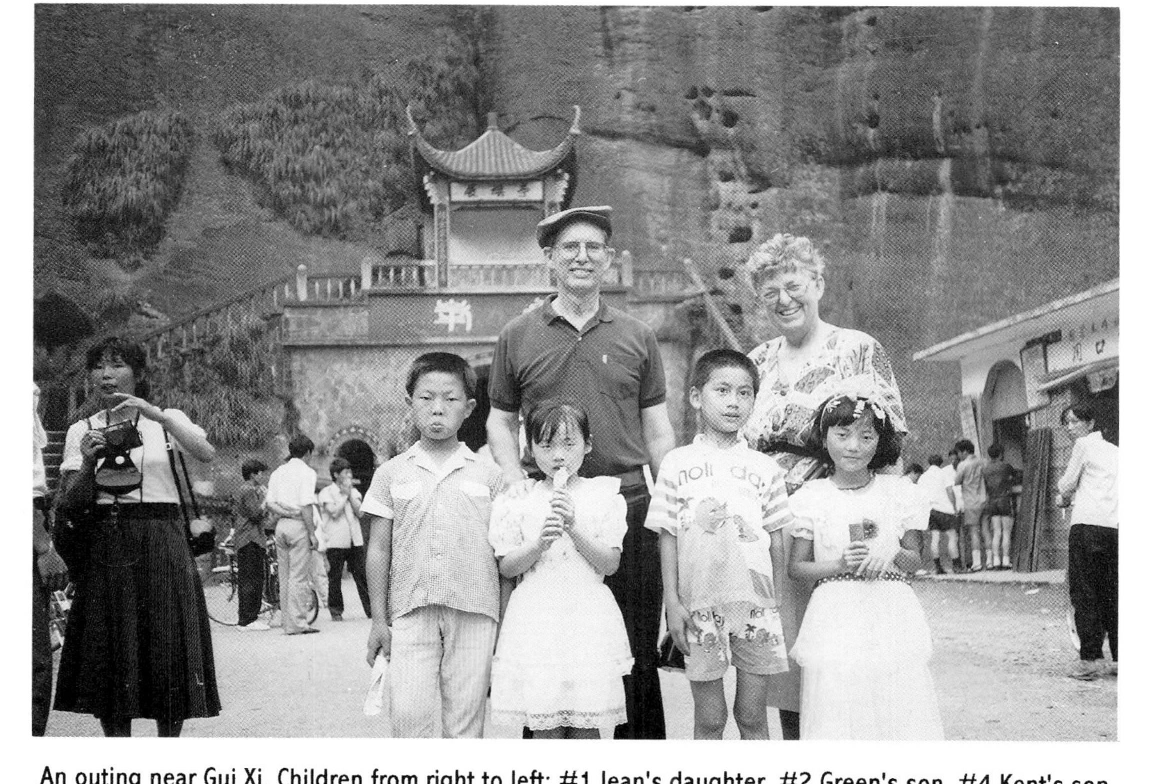

An outing near Gui Xi. Children from right to left: #1 Jean's daughter, #2 Green's son, #4 Kent's son.

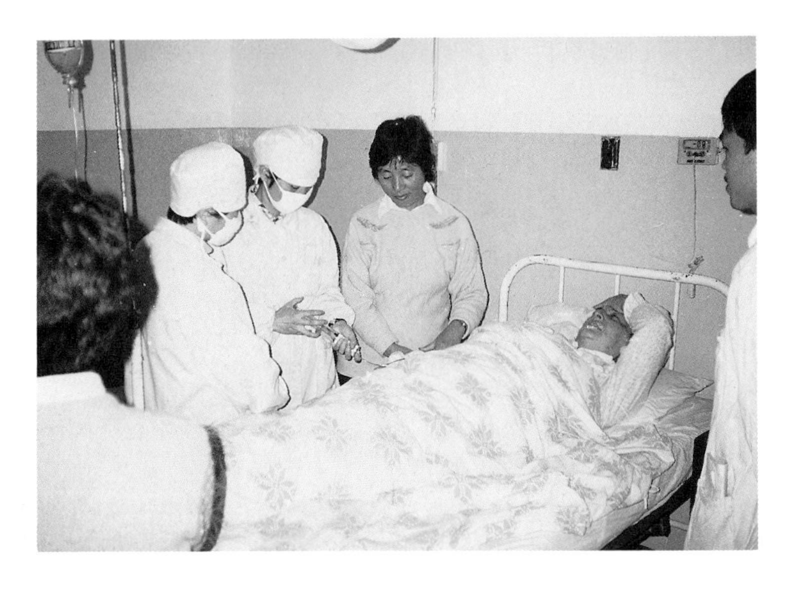

Leona receives glucose I.V. in Nanchang Hospital while her student holds her hand.

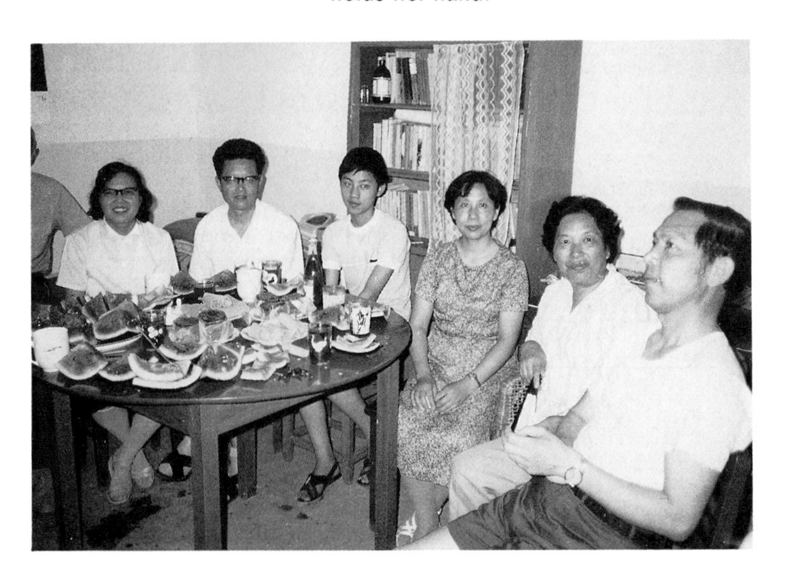

Farewell watermelon party with Nanjing colleagues.

Leona's conversation class sings "Santa Claus is Coming to Town," at the Christmas Party.

Pastor James Wang is in the front row. The young pastors, to whom we taught English, are in the back row.

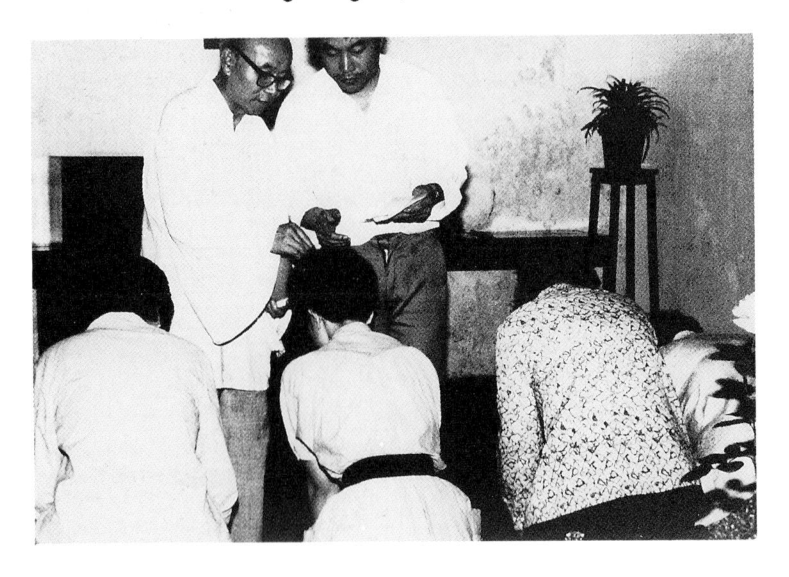

Esther's baptism.

Green re-enforces the top of the Christmas Tree with a chop stick. Our students made the paper.

Leona and the usher who saved us seats at Nanchang Union Church.

Junior Middle School students in Wangli, suburb of Nanchang, follow us across the campus.

Chinese employees assemble Bibles at the Amity Printing Plant near Nanjing.

A store manager and his friends in Hoh Hot, Inner Mongolia. Xu Qing Mei, the attorney, is standing next to me.

Dragon boats practicing for Dragon Boat Festival races. Paddlers will keep in time with their boat's drum beat.

Language. The tape portrayed different English teaching methods, but the setting for each method presented was an American classroom. The thirty teacher-audience enjoyed the slide show of the United States. They also appreciated the exposure to new teaching methods. I felt they were particularly impressed, however, with the scenes of American classrooms. It was not just the carpeting, the new furniture, and the many shelves of books. American classrooms are so colorful. The furniture and cabinets are painted bright colors and the walls are covered with bright pictures, and posters, and bulletin board displays. They have a different look from most Chinese classrooms. We returned to the reception room and ate bay berries and lotus seeds served in a sweet syrup. They were very tasty.

Leona developed bronchitis and was suffering from wheezing, congestion, and a low-grade fever. It was her turn to lecture. I reviewed her speech in case I had to present it for her. At the last minute, however, Leona crawled out of bed, dragged herself to the college, and gave a two hour lecture. As soon as she finished, she went straight to the doctor's office. I stayed in the auditorium and handled the question/answer period. Leona and I have felt that one of our strengths is the fact that we are a team. When each of us gives a lecture, it is far more effective than if either of us gave two lectures. That is why Leona had made such an effort to present her own lecture. Chinese people are organized and methodical. They appreciate lectures or essays that are based on a one-two-three-four structure. Leona had structured her talk on A-E-I-O-U, since all of her audience were English majors or English teachers. She was speaking on the A, B, C's of American Basic Characteristics, and stated that Americans were Adventurous, Enterprising, Independent, Outspoken, and Unexpectedly generous. The audience loved it. She said that much of America was settled by immigrants, and many of those immigrants were the Adventurous ones; the not so adventurous stayed at home. After analyzing American characteristics according to her A, E, I, O, and U, she then told about our family, our three married children, and how they had been adventurous in their frequent moves and job-changes and so forth. Chinese people wherever we went were interested in Americans and American culture.

Leona has served as a pre-school director in the United States, so she did not want to miss the visit to the local kindergarten. Fortified by her newly prescribed medicine, she went on the afternoon tour. The kindergarten had three hundred children aged four, five, and six. We were met by the director, taken to the reception room for our cup of tea, and the director gave us the statistics and described the program.

The students were assembled in outdoor activity and interest groups with about ten pupils in each group. One group danced and marched in time to the music played on a pump organ. One group wore paper hats with pictures of cats and held fishing poles with magnets instead of hooks, trying to catch paper fish with metal buttons. We took a picture of a group of children holding poles with fire crackers tied to the end of their lines. Lighted punks were stuck in the sand. The hand-eye coordination exercise was touching the fuse of the fire cracker to the lighted punk. One girl in our picture had faith in their success; she held her hands over her ears. Leona loved the visit. She was able to compare their equipment, their activities, and their program with things she had done in California. She danced with one group and played catch with another group.

The delegation of college dignitaries that were with us were happy to see Leona so excited, and the college photographer and the city television crew were enthusiastic as well. With all of the Chinese photography, I was surprised when the kindergarten director asked for copies of the pictures that I was taking. I sent all of my slide film to the United States for processing, but I had prints made of that visit and later sent the pictures to the director.

Leona's energy was gone after this excursion, so she asked to be taken back to the hotel. I continued on to the next site, the Number One Primary school, where I was met by the principal and other leaders. I was still accompanied by the college president, the dean, the foreign affairs officer, two teachers, and a photographer. We went to the reception room for tea and a formal introduction to the school. Then we visited a fourth grade class. As we entered the room, fifty boys and girls clapped their hands. On cue, they all raised their books and pretended to be reading. I looked at my watch. It was now five o'clock. In such a disciplined class I was surprised to see all the boys wearing red baseball caps. When I looked closer, I was even more surprised; on the front of each cap, in large white letters, it read 'Marlboro.' This saddened me. As an educator we have worked so hard over the years to discourage our American students from smoking. As we turned to leave the classroom, all the students clapped again.

We then visited a special class where five students were receiving instruction in calligraphy. I went up to one student and took his picture as he was making bold brush strokes with black ink. One of the school leaders said, "Oh, the best student is that one at the end of the table." I went over to watch his work, and my interpreter said that he was writing "Peace and friendship." I realized that that was probably for me, which in fact it was, so I had to take a few more pictures. Then someone used my camera to photograph the eleven year old student presenting his special calligraphy to me. I asked one of my hosts, "What time do the students go home?" She said, "They will go home after you leave."

We then visited a small auditorium. There were about thirty girls in costume. As we arrived they sang a greeting song and then Jingle Bells. Then ten first and second graders did a dance, and then the third and fourth graders danced, and finally the fifth and sixth grade girls danced. They were very cute in their bright yellow costumes and big smiles. I took several pictures while they were dancing. When they finished, the whole group re-assembled and insisted that I have my picture taken with them. The program was over about five thirty. As we were leaving, I could see the students running off the campus. They were normally finished at four twenty, but had waited for my visit.

Saturday morning Leona was feeling much better. The Chinese medicine was working. We were asked to meet with two first year English classes. Leona met with one for an hour and I with the other; then we switched classes. When we finished, the students insisted that they have their pictures taken with us. Leona and I sat at the teacher's desk in the front of the room and all who could gather around us, sitting and standing, did so. They took three pictures, photographing one third of the students in each picture. Then we went to the other room and repeated the process. We had an extra hour in our morning schedule, so Leona and I were able to go to my student's home, the one who had made the arrangements for us to visit his college. We met his wife, his mother-in-law, and his seven year old son. We had a delightful visit and as we were leaving, he and one of his colleagues gave us gifts—two pieces of silk, about one and a half meters each, one was sky blue, and the other shocking pink.

Saturday afternoon was the climax of the three-day lecture tour. I was scheduled to give a two hour lecture on "Analytical Thinking, a Necessity for Chinese Modernization." Leona would then present a summary of her lecture from the previous day. The auditorium had seating for six hundred people. The college had issued invitations to all of the teachers of English in the surrounding eight counties, but people could come 'by ticket only' because of the limited seating. The college had been so impressed with Leona's lecture the day before, they asked if she would try to summarize it and present the essence in a fifteen minute speech following my anticipated two-hour lecture.

The college president was introduced first. Then the foreign affairs officer for the city was invited to speak. Chinese speakers can be very flowery. He stated that it had been his responsibility to decide whether the Damerons should come to Yanchen. He said that he had been reluctant to allow it, but had finally agreed that we could come. He then said, "But after meeting the Damerons, and hearing their fine lectures, may I say now, that they are welcome to come to our city any time they want to." It was time to present our lectures. Then the audience was invited to submit written questions.

I could not believe their patience on Saturday afternoon. The president concluded the afternoon with an elaborate thank-you, and then presented Leona and me with gifts, a cloisonne vase and an art scroll. I responded with a can of fancy-pack California almonds and a brochure on California. The program had lasted for three hours. It had been an exhilarating and exhausting experience. As we watched the six hundred people leave, we could not help wondering, "What do they think?" We were the only Americans they had ever met. Our reflections were, "We were pioneers; others will follow."[1]

That evening in our hotel we watched the television coverage of our visit to Yanchen. It showed our talking with the first year class, but it did not report on our visit to the kindergarten. It had been a long three days.

New Year's in Jingdezhen

Ping was thirty-four, assertive and friendly. Before saying, "Good morning," she would walk up close, grasp my arm, smile, and then greet me. Ping was the top student in the slower conversation class. When I called on someone in class and they hesitated, Ping called out the answer. Her clothes were more colorful than the other students' clothes,

---

[1] The Amity Foundation, our sponsoring body, did send a couple to Nantong Teachers College the following year and to Yanchen beginning two years later.

and she wore a different outfit every day. She told us privately, "I'm rich."

Ping and another student, Lancelot, both taught middle school in Jingdezhen, an historical porcelain manufacturing city. Shortly before Christmas Ping asked Leona and me, "Why don't you come and visit us over New Year's?" The idea sounded interesting, but we did not consider it seriously until her husband attended our class Christmas party, and repeated the invitation. "You can stay at our house." Very few foreigners have the opportunity of staying overnight in a Chinese home. The government discourages it; the leaders do not want foreigners to get too close to Chinese citizens and spawn discontent. When the director of our Training Center heard that we were planning to go to Jingdezhen, he tried to discourage us. He said that it would be very cold, traveling this time of year. He said the roads would be wet and traveling would be dangerous. At first we did not understand why he was so concerned at our going. Was he in agreement with the government officials and trying to keep us from staying in a private home? When we were not dissuaded from going, the director called Lancelot to his office and in a very serious tone said, "You will go with them; you will be responsible for their safety." Now we understood. Since we were assigned to his university, Director Xu was responsible for us. On this trip there would be no foreign affairs officer, and no university officials to receive us in Jingdezhen. Director Xu wanted to make sure there were no problems.

We were up at six thirty. Leona had baked a loaf of bread, and we made sandwiches with spread from a care package we had received from home. It had stopped raining during the night, but there was standing water everywhere. We walked to the university gate to meet Lancelot, our Chinese student who would accompany us. I was wearing my backpack and carrying a plastic bag with oranges, bananas, sandwiches and a Pepsi bottle of drinking water.

There were about thirty-five people already waiting at the local bus stop. When the bus arrived, it was already full.

I thought there was no way that all of us could get on, but we did. I saw an inch of space; I pushed and squeezed out four or five inches—but then I still had my backpack.

When the local bus started, I was standing in the aisle, completely surrounded by bodies. I am only five feet ten, but in China I can see above most of the people around me. At that height my head touched the roof of the bus. I was too tall to look out the windows; I had a great angle shot of the curbs and gutters all the way to the Inter-city bus station.

The Inter-city bus station waiting room was large with comfortable wooden park-like benches. A crippled man came by on crutches, begging a few coins from each of the waiting passengers. We did not give him anything. The government is trying to discourage begging, and we do not want foreigners to be identified as the soft touch. Our student gave him a few coins. Then a woman carrying a small child and dressed like a peasant from the countryside approached Leona for a handout. Leona said, "No," but she persisted. Finally our Chinese student shooed her away. Five minutes later she returned and went straight to Leona and would not leave. Finally our student took her by the arm, and more aggressively told her to leave. He then gave her a coin and other Chinese bystanders started talking to her as well, and she finally left.

The long distance bus that we would ride for our seven hour trip to Jingdezhen was called an "air" bus. It had reserved seats with high backs, some heat, and a stereo. We were not sure why it was called an **air** bus until we started moving and then Leona figured it out—it had an air horn. If that is really not the reason, there was considerable empirical evidence supporting that theory. The bus did have several Chinese characteristics—narrow seats so close together our knees touched the seat back in front of us, the net storage bag was filled with yesterday's orange peels, passengers spit on the floor, and all the men smoked. The overhead baggage racks were about five inches deep, so I kept my backpack and plastic bag between and under my knees.

After a couple hours we came to a railroad crossing with the barrier down. The bus stopped and while we were waiting, two male passengers jumped out and urinated in plain sight along the side of the bus. We made a restaurant stop at one fifteen. There were two open rooms (by open I mean there was no wall on one side), with small tables for dining. A third room had a double bed and was probably the cook's bedroom. There were no other buildings around; we were right out in the middle of the countryside. Two farmers were trying to drive a two-hundred-fifty pound pig down the road. Three or four women were washing some clothes in a ditch across the road. Our student had warned us to bring our own lunch. Some of the passengers went into the restaurant, but many did not. About one hundred feet away there was an out house made of hewn stone. The rumor was that the bus driver was paid fifty yuan for stopping at this particular restaurant. We suspected there was some reason other than the food.

The assistant driver found some pork to buy. He carried a hunk that would weigh about thirty-five pounds back onto the bus and plopped it on a shelf against the windshield with no paper or wrapper of any kind. When the bus resumed its journey, bouncing along the road, the pork just lay there and sort of quivered for the next four hours.

The Chinese countryside is fascinating to look at. We saw old men herding flocks of thirty ducks along the road, women washing clothes in sloughs, and water buffalo relaxing during the off season. In the little villages I was always impressed to see pigs running loose like pet dogs. A Chinese told me, "They are the freest things in all of China." Since it was a rainy day, we also saw two trucks and one cargo tricycle overturned and lying on their sides in the drainage ditch.

After an interesting, but tiring trip we arrived in Jingdezhen about five thirty and were met by our host with a car. He does not own a car, but knew a driver who was willing to help out "as a friend." They took us to our host's home, a new two bedroom one-story house owned by Ping's unit, the Number One Middle School. The house was actually a duplex, two houses side by side with a single red tile roof extending over both units. No house in China has a garage because no one has a car. There was a graveled space in front of the collection of houses, but there was no driveway. There were a few trees, but no formal landscaping. Ping said she would plant a few vegetables in the spring.

The house had two large bedrooms, about ten by twelve each, a modest living room, a dining room, and a small kitchen. The floors were bare cement except for the master bed room. Bob, Ping's husband, and Nancy, Ping's English name, had just laid a carpet in their bedroom, probably because we were coming. The carpet was very nice, but un-stretched and without a pad. There was no heat in the home, and the indoor temperature was about fifty degrees. We had anticipated the lack of heat by wearing two layers of long underwear. Nancy was wearing a down jacket inside her home. In the kitchen there was a cement sink with a cold water tap, the only running water in the house. There was a charcoal stove to heat water in a tea kettle, and a two-burner stove fed by bottled butane gas. There was no bathroom, but there was a small room, perhaps three and a half by four and a half feet with a potty for nighttime use. During the daytime we walked about one hundred yards to a relatively clean, non-flushing, community toilet. The neighborhood toilet is a great equalizer. As you walk past six squatters, separated only by three-foot cement dividers, and take your place in the seventh spot, the common phrase, "He puts his pants on one leg at a time" seems so inadequate.

Bob and Nancy had a five year old son who they farmed out to the maternal grandmother's for the evening. Bob's mother lived with them, but was also somewhere else that evening; we were given the master bedroom, and I assume Bob and Nancy used his mother's room. While we were visiting, Nancy's older sister was in the kitchen cooking dinner. She had been asked to help cook to allow Nancy more time to serve as hostess. They set two small plates, about three-inches in diameter, on the table and asked us to sit down. The chairs were ceramic barrel shaped stools covered with fabric caps to make them warmer in the winter. They were beautiful with the famille rose patterns we would see in the shops and museums the next day. We were embarrassed to sit at the table and eat by ourselves, but Bob insisted. After about five minutes, however, he sat down and began to eat, but very sparingly. Every few minutes, Nancy would bring in another dish of food. There was a knock at the door. It was Bob's brother. After introductions he joined us at the table and ate heartily. Nancy joined us too. When we had almost finished and the last dish had been served, Nancy's sister also sat with us and ate. They then topped off their dinner with a big bowl of noodles and all ate enthusiastically.

About nine o'clock Bob changed to his outdoor shoes, added another coat, and went by bicycle to his mother-in-law's to pick up Zsa Zsa, the five year old son. On his return, after a very brief period of shyness, Zsa Zsa entertained us until it was time for bed.

Bob said, "In China, before we go to bed, we wash our face and our feet." He poured water from the teakettle into a wash basin and I washed my face. I asked for a towel, and he said, "Just wring out the wash cloth." I then repeated the routine for my feet, and we went to bed.

The bedroom was beautiful. There were attractive drapes on the windows, a nice looking full height corner cabinet—there are no built-in closets—and wedding pictures hanging over the bed displaying bride and groom in western dress. For bedding we had two heavy comforters and the pillows were filled with rice hulls. We slept warm and comfortably.

Although population figures vary according to whom you talk to, the city of Jingdezhen had about six hundred thousand people and was, therefore, smaller than our city,

Nanchang, which had about one million. We did not hear a sound during the night, and the next morning were awakened by a rooster crowing. We had a nice breakfast of hot fresh milk—Leona told them not to put any sugar in ours, very fried eggs, and fried *jiaozis* (boiled *jiaozis* or dumplings were left over from the evening before and then fried for breakfast.) We appreciated the fresh milk since we only got powdered milk at home in Nanchang. Zsa Zsa slept in and did not join us for breakfast.

Whenever a foreigner stays overnight in a different city, he must register with the Security Affairs Office. When we arrived we reminded our host that we had to register, and he said he had already taken care of it. After breakfast, however, we were informed that Security was very nervous about our staying in a private home, and the only reason we got permission for the first night was that our host had told them we would be very tired from our journey, etc. Now it seemed expected that we would transfer to the local hotel, but they reassured us it was a four star hotel and that was the place where all the foreign guests stayed. While walking me to the neighborhood toilet, our host said he was sorry we could not stay with them that night. I asked, "Is it because of the June fourth incident?" (the government suppressed student protests on June 4, 1989, in Tiananmen Square). He responded, "Probably." Then he added, "When you come to visit us again, after some time has passed, you will be able to stay with us in our home next time."

A car arrived. This was a different car, a different friend. The city of Jingdezhen is the historic Chinese porcelain city where the ancient process of porcelain was discovered seventeen hundred years ago in the Han Dynasty. Today porcelain is called *China* or *Chinaware*, and there are one hundred porcelain factories in Jingdezhen. We visited several museums—buildings built four hundred years ago during the Ming Dynasty, housing porcelain shards from almost one thousand years ago. Then we visited an old porcelain factory where workmen were just removing vases from a kiln that was still warm. The vases were in clay cylindrical pots. We watched a young woman pick up each vase and break off the base plate used during firing, and then saw workmen wrap the new vases in straw for transport. We went to a museum display area, but since it was New Year's Day, it was locked. Our host knew somebody, keys were produced, and the door was unlocked for our private showing. We saw blue and white porcelain. We saw famille rose and rice pattern. We saw vases higher than our heads and other vases as thin as egg shells. There were price tags with prices as high as thirty-eight thousand yuan. Some of the vases and cups and bowls and plates were old, some were modern, but they were all beautiful.

We went back to Bob and Nancy's home for lunch. We had pork chops, cold roast beef, soup, rice, mushrooms on green vegetable, quail eggs and cooked celery, scrambled egg jiaozis, fish, and a dish of hot peppers. For beverage they served wine. Zsa Zsa walked around, entertained the guests, and then climbed onto a chair and poured some wine—mostly on the table. He acted like American five year old's. The parents were very tolerant. Nancy simply took a rag and started wiping up the mess and never said anything to Zsa Zsa. We took several pictures of Zsa Zsa. After lunch Nancy's parents arrived. We took more pictures. Zsa Zsa stood on his head on the couch. We took more pictures. We all seemed reluctant for all of this to end—from there we would be checking into the hotel.

A car arrived; it was the same friend as the day before. He drove us to the hotel. Bob said the price would be two hundred yuan—that's high. Bob talked with the young man at the desk. He was one of Bob's former students. I could not follow what was said, but when I signed the register, he said the price was one hundred forty yuan, which was still more than a middle school teacher's monthly salary.

We left our things at the hotel and walked down to the center of town, about three-fourth's of a mile. It was raining off and on. In the middle of town there is a street they call Porcelain Street. There were rows of shops on both sides for one hundred yards that sell nothing but porcelain. In front of all these shops, there are free market vendors with their porcelain "seconds" and "thirds" displayed on the sidewalk. They displayed Buddhas, and plates, statues and vases, cups and bowls and spoons. Our host took us into a shop where higher quality porcelain was sold. Since he was a government inspector for porcelain being exported, he carefully examined our intended purchases and rejected a tea set we had admired, showing us the handle had been broken. We did buy a lovely flower vase with a famille rose design.

Bob then walked us back to the hotel, apologizing that his friends with cars were not available. He then walked back downtown and caught a bus to his home.

We appreciated the chance to stay in a private home and recognized in this post June Fourth climate what a privilege it had been. But there is a certain amount of strain living in an unfamiliar environment when you are trying so hard not to offend. We were glad to be in a hotel, a more neutral setting, all by ourselves, so we could relax for a couple of hours. Suddenly there was a knock on the door. It was Mary, a middle school teacher and a friend of Nancy's whom we had met earlier in the day. She knew we were in the hotel by ourselves and had made a special effort to join us so we would not be lonely. Aaagh! Mary was aged thirty-three, attractive, enthusiastic, and looking forward to the dance that would begin at eight o'clock in the hotel. Her husband was a doctor and "watched television pictures of people, and helped analyze what was wrong with their head or chest." Mary's English was pretty good, but we still lost a lot in the translation. Anyway, her husband was working back in Nanchang for a few days, so she was joining us for New Year's Eve. We had a nice visit with Mary. We found out that her salary after teaching for ten years in the middle school was eighty-three yuan per month, about sixteen U. S. dollars, and that it was the same as last year's. Her rent was three yuan per month, but she paid an additional three yuan for water and about seven-fifty yuan for electricity. Her electricity bill was high because she had an iron, radio, refrigerator, washing machine, rice cooker, and a television. She cooked with gas. She had an eight year old boy and paid twenty yuan per term tuition which included the cost of the books.

Bob arrived at eight o'clock so we could all go to the dance. He carried a plastic bag with a bar of soap and a cloth.

He explained, "After the dance I will take a bath in your hotel bath tub. Since we do not have a bathroom in our house, I have not had a chance to take a bath for a long time. I am looking forward to taking one here."

"Great! Help yourself. By the way, Where's Nancy?"

"She's in the bar waiting for the manager. She knows the manager and if she gets a chance to talk to him, she may be able to get a better price for your room."

In China it takes friends to ride in a car, get into a museum on a holiday, get a reduced price in a hotel—maybe even to stay in a private home. *Guan xi* is everywhere. It definitely is "Who you know," in China.

We did not see any other foreigners in that four star hotel except a small group of Japanese. There were perhaps one hundred people at the dance, mostly young Chinese who came to the hotel just for the dance. The taped music was supplemented by a female vocalist. The predominant music was waltzes and disco and the dance floor was crowded. When there was a fast beat, however, young men and some young women as well danced individually or in couples of the same sex. The lighted mirror ball and rotating colored lights added to the festive atmosphere. I danced with Leona, I danced with Nancy, I danced with Mary. When I was exhausted and sat down, Mary would come and ask me to dance again. We really did have fun. It was a glorious New Year's Eve. Then suddenly, at ten-thirty, the lights came on; the dance was over. We all returned to the hotel room and Bob took his bath.

Bob found a friend to drive us to the train station the next morning. Leona had sandwich spread, but we needed to buy a loaf of bread. We stopped at a vendor cart, but Bob would not hear of it. He said Nancy had brought a lunch for us. Even though our train tickets were for hard seat, we were directed toward the soft seat waiting room because we were foreigners. When the train arrived dozens of Chinese, mostly young men, crowded around the train car door, all trying to force their way aboard. There are no reserved seats in hard seat class and people were very aggressive in trying to get a seat. I joined the group jostling toward the steps, but felt like a piece of drift wood in rapids, and soon found myself back in the eddy of the stream. My host called to me and said not to try to get on. At that point, Lancelot recognized a former student already on the train who opened a window and helped him climb in through the window; he then laid claim to seats for us.

The seats were full, the aisle was full, and the train started. When you ride hard seat, people take what they need for the trip: thermoses or jars of tea, oranges, watermelon seeds, bananas, and cigarettes—lots of cigarettes. Most Chinese men smoke and they smoke everywhere. Although Chinese like fresh air, in the middle of winter in an unheated train, they keep the windows closed most of the time. We opened our window every time the train slowed down to let out some of the smoke. A vendor pushed his way through the aisle selling sugar cane. Many passengers bought the eighteen inch pieces, chewed out the juice, and spit the pulp on the floor, along with the watermelon seeds, the orange peels, and part of the banana peels. The rest of the garbage was thrown out the window. Around twelve o'clock a vendor came through selling little styro-foam boxes of rice/vegetables. All of these containers were thrown out of the window also; when we rode the bus parallel to the railroad tracks, we had seen the eight foot wide litter pattern two days before.

Eventually one needs to go to the toilet; although you postpone it as long as you can. I had great difficulty even walking—walking? down the aisle through all of the people standing, leaning, half-sitting. When someone stands in an aisle for several hours, one becomes rather permanent.

When I got to the toilet it was occupied, of course. When there are that many people riding in the same train car, all of the facilities are over taxed. When I was able to go in, it was a typical Chinese toilet—no seat. There is a slot in the floor about six inches wide which one straddles. Paper is never provided. There was a small metal sink about eight inches in diameter, but the sink leaked and there was a half inch of water on the floor and unfortunately my right boot leaked.

About twelve-thirty I suggested it was time for lunch. Nancy had brought a wide-mouthed thermos. It was filled with rice, steaming hot, and in the top tray was sliced ox stomach. She had also brought three ceramic spoons, but as she unwrapped them, they fell on the table and two of them broke. I produced an enamel cup. Nancy filled it with rice and some ox stomach, handed it to Leona with the one good spoon and Leona ate while we watched. The ox stomach was a little tough, but the flavor was much better than it sounds. Then Nancy refilled the cup, carefully wiped off the spoon with a piece of notebook paper, we accepted this now as standard procedure, and handed it to me. I ate, being careful to clean up everything before handing the cup and spoon to Nancy. Nancy repeated this operation and she ate.

Riding hard seat is a public activity. The people standing in the aisle become part of your party. One young man proved to be a junior at our university and after a brief self-introduction produced an English work book, and asked if I would help him with the exercises. When I tired of this, he did not leave—where could he go? He had become part of our group. When I needed to go to the toilet again, I got up and started picking my way through the crowds in the aisle. I felt someone shoving me from behind. It was my new student benefactor trying to get in front of me. I had little choice and let him squeeze past me. Then he pushed and shoved and asked authoritatively for people to move aside so I could get through. I was embarrassed. Chinese "friends" are very solicitous, and they seem more pushy when they have a foreigner in tow. I would have preferred to have been unobtrusive and inconspicuous.

We arrived in Nanchang at five-fifteen, right on time. I felt this was rather remarkable since the train had been thirty minutes late in Jingdezhen. We collected our things and got off the train. We did not go into the station, but started walking down the tracks toward our university. There were probably fifty people, mostly students, all going the same direction. Nancy and Lancelot spotted two of their former students and asked them to help us carry our parcels and bags. We entered an alley, walked a quarter of a mile to the main street, and then back to our university home. It had been a very interesting week-end. We were tired. We were glad to get home, but we realized we had just experienced a series of events that are just not available until *After the Tour Bus Leaves.*

Killed by Kindness

The middle school teachers finished their year of refresher classes the end of May. Then they returned to their communities and their schools in order to try out their new techniques and newly developed skills in a month of student teaching. We traveled by train to two of these communities to observe several of the students' teaching. Since the trips were organized by the Training Center, we were accompanied by an administrative assistant who made all of the arrangements. He bought the tickets, brought a bag of fruit, helped carry our luggage, and took care of us on the train. Between our escort, our students, and the community leaders who received us, we were, in fact, killed by kindness.

It was late June in southeastern China and it was hot and muggy. The ceiling fans and the open train windows, however, made the soft seat car relatively comfortable. The fields of rice were almost ready for harvest. Peasants were irrigating their fields using dippers and wooden buckets suspended from carry poles. On the train we played Running Fast, a Chinese card game, with the young administrative assistant. Since we were just learning the card game, Chinese strangers in near-by seats enjoyed looking over our shoulders and telling us what to play. As we traveled the four and a half hour ride to Gui Xi, we also read, and ate watermelon seeds, typical Chinese pastimes. Gui Xi was a smallish town with no apparent western influence. It was off the tourist route, and there were very few foreign products in any of the shops. Three of our students were student teaching in middle schools in Gui Xi, and we would observe their classes. We were also invited to lecture on teaching methodology to all of the teachers of English from the three middle schools in town.

We were met by all three of our students, the head of the educational bureau for the city, and one of the school administrators. We were taken to the educational bureau's private restaurant and served a welcome banquet. We had ten or twelve dishes. The beverage was warm beer and Chinese Seven-up which was also served warm. The food was good, but we were most impressed with all of the toasts to everyone's health, success, and friendship.

The tourist hotel where we would be staying was located about two miles out of town. Our three students and the two leaders went with us in the mini-van. At the hotel, motivated by helpfulness, everyone had to carry something, if not the suitcase, then one of the two little cloth carry bags with our plastic water bottles.

Our hotel suite had a bed room and a sitting room. Everyone sat down except me. They insisted that I sit down.

I said, "I have been riding on a train for almost five hours, then sitting in a restaurant, and then sitting in a car. I would prefer to stand up for a while."

But who pays any attention to logic. One of my students got up, and while insisting that I sit down, grabbed me by the arm to forcefully pull me toward a chair. Finally I sat down so that *they could rest.*

About five minutes later everyone left with the admonition, "Now you must rest!"

We had gone to Gui Xi to observe our students' teaching, to lecture to English teachers, and to do whatever else was required, but all we had done up to that point was eat. But now we would rest for two hours.

At four o'clock we toured the copper smelter plant. It was a modern plant, built only five years before as a joint-venture project with Japan. We wore hard hats. We watched as a furnace was opened, with fiery sparks spewing forth. We walked along row after row of eight-hundred pound copper slabs. The facility is the largest copper smelter plant in China, producing twenty thousand tons of copper, eighty-five thousand tons of sulfuric acid, plus gold and silver each year. The plant employed three thousand people. We were most impressed by the control room, however, where there was a fifty foot wall of computer screens and dials, gauges and knobs. The plant was an example of China's recent efforts toward modernization.

There were many Chinese guests eating in the large hotel dining room. We said we would be happy to eat there. Our escort said, "Our food has been set up for us in another room." So the three of us had a quiet dinner in a private dining room. Foreigners are generally kept separate from the Chinese guests. After dinner we walked around the hotel grounds. We were two miles from town and there was no transportation. It was hot and muggy, but the large hotel swimming pool was dry. We went to bed early.

The next morning we went to the Number One Middle School to observe Jean's seventh grade English class. The classroom was on the second floor, and as we climbed the cement stairs, students crowded around us, saying, "Hello," and smiled. I stopped and asked one a question. He backed away, too shy to try out his English. So I shook his hand.

Then everyone wanted to shake hands; I felt like I was running for office.

Several town and school dignitaries accompanied us into Jean's classroom and we made an imposing row of visitors in the back of her class of sixty pupils. The students sat very close together at desks that were old and cracked and worn. The walls were cement with occasional notices pasted directly on the wall; there were no bulletin boards. The blackboard on the front wall was of poor quality. Some of the fluorescent lights did not work. All of the windows were open and it was hot. Jean did not seem nervous with all of the visitors. She included many different activities, including several techniques that we had taught. She was teaching a lesson on superlatives. She wrote "tall, taller, tallest" on the board. She called three pupils to the front of the room and said, "Wang is tall, Ming is taller, and Chen is the tallest." She used three more students for comparative ages, and four more students for arranging proper word order in a sentence. We were proud of her use of students in the class activities. It was at this level, seventh grade, that Chinese pupils begin the study of English and the class was very interested and responsive.

Green's seventh grade class was also lively. He used a variety of activities, including T.P.R. (Total Physical Response), asking half the class to stand and respond to his commands while the other students observed, and then he switched to the other half. He involved individual students at several other points in the lesson as well. The local leaders were impressed with the new command of English and the new teaching methods demonstrated by their teachers after they had studied at the Training Center in Nanchang for a year.

We spoke informally to a group of seniors, in English and without an interpreter. Most of the students must have understood because many of them asked questions afterwards. The English teachers from the school joined us for a group picture.

The campus was surrounded by a brick wall. There was a formal entrance which was closed at night. A tour of the campus included several two-story brick classroom buildings, and a large pond with a lovely fountain.

Lunch was a banquet. The center attraction was the six inch turtle floating in a bowl of soup. The sight of it was a little unnerving. Then someone reached into the bowl and tore it apart with chop sticks, and placed generous portions on our plates. After we got over the shock of eating our first turtle, we really liked it. The turtle was followed by squid, eel, whole frogs, pine nuts with fish bits, quail eggs, a dish of hot peppers, dumplings filled with pork, hollow green stems, sliced tomatoes covered with sugar, pork slices and rice. Chinese eat very little meat in their daily diet, but when a banquet is served, it is mostly meat. The beverages for the banquet were beer and a Chinese version of 7-Up, both served at room temperature. Tea is considered too plain to be served with meals. The dinner was hosted by the Number One Middle School, and dozens of bottles of beer and cans of 7-Up were consumed in toasts.

We wanted to go downtown, just to look around. We never dreamed how complicated that would be. The streets were narrow. They looked like a Chinese version of a flea market. There were rows of permanent stores and little shops, but spilling out onto the sidewalk and into the street itself were small tables with goods and produce.

I started to cross the little street. Our student, Green, a man aged forty, took me by the arm to help me across. I felt this was very unnecessary because there were no vehicles at all, except for an occasional bicycle or cart. We walked between and around baskets of plums, local tobacco, displays of hand tools and hardware items, both new and used. Artisans were weaving bamboo products and pounding and shaping metal buckets and pots.

Leona walked ahead with two women, Jean, and the vice-principal, on either side of her. I followed about ten feet behind, walking between Green and our interpreter. The driver and two other male teachers walked on our flanks, like secret service agents for the President. Whenever anyone walked near us they shooed them over a few feet. When one man innocently started to walk between Leona and me, one of them grabbed the stranger by the arm and made him walk around us. A boy came towards us riding a bicycle. One of the men grabbed the handle bars, stopped him, then re-directed him away from us. We were a bit dismayed by all of this protection. This was our second year in China. In Nanjing and again in Nanchang we rode bicycles all over the city by ourselves and walked wherever we pleased. This certainly was not an unsafe neighborhood. We also were not security threats. We do not speak Chinese well enough to talk intimately with the local Chinese. Our conclusion was, that when you are the host, you have an extremely high sense of responsibility and a high sense of hospitality, and this translates into over-protection.

Foreigners are extremely rare in that town, and we were terribly conspicuous just by being there, but we were greatly troubled at the impression being created by our hosts. I am sensitive to the stereotype that all Americans are wealthy, and pampered. Chinese people say, "The Big Noses have privileges," and our treatment did not lessen that image.

It was a very hot day and although there were many trees, we were walking in and out of the shade. Green decided it was too hot for us, and that we should both have umbrellas. He ran back to one of the shops and got two used umbrellas that we were obligated to use. This made us feel even more ridiculous.

We stopped at a woodworking work shop. Our whole entourage crowded into the small room. It was still *xiu xi* time so the proprietor was asleep on a cot. They woke him up and asked him to demonstrate his craft. He sorted through his wood, selected a piece, and fitted it into a very old lathe. As he worked, we all crowded around and watched. Someone sent out for drinks and soon, bottles of warm Chinese orange soda were being opened. The craftsman carved a lamp base with a free-floating wooden ring, and presented it to us as a gift. We thanked him profusely, and we all marched out.

Out on the street we could hear the beat of a drum. It came from the river where the dragon boats were practicing for the Dragon Boat Festival boat races that would be held on Sunday. I had never seen dragon boats before. I handed my umbrella to someone, and raced down the river bank before someone decided that I had to hold their hand, and started taking pictures. The boats were large. Each one holds about thirty paddlers plus a drummer to beat out the timing of the strokes. Each boat represents a different village from the surrounding area and the paddlers are generally peasants. They were very colorful in their red bandanna sweat bands. When I took their picture, the paddlers smiled and waved. Then the paddlers in the next boat wanted their picture taken too. After several pictures, I was a "good boy" and walked sedately back up the bank, carrying my umbrella.

Our third student, Kent, taught an eleventh grade class at Number Two Middle School. We had taught from the senior middle school text book at Jiangxi Teachers University and were familiar with the lesson he presented. We enjoyed his class, but it was obvious that eleventh grade students are not nearly as interested in learning English as the seventh grade students were in the several classes we had visited. We wondered if this drop in interest were the result of their teaching nothing but grammar year after year after year. They focus on grammar because that is what will be on the college entrance examination.

Following the class observation, we went to Kent's apartment, accompanied by several government and school officials. His wife piled the coffee table high with bananas and oranges and then implored everyone to eat several. She also served watermelon. Watermelon is one food that Chinese do not eat with chop sticks. In fact, they do not use any utensil at all. The hostess placed several dish pans on the floor, and we shared these in two's and three's as a place to spit our seeds. The juice went on the floor, but fortunately it was a bare cement floor. I thought, what an interesting photo that would make—all of us, including the government and school leaders, enjoying our watermelon and spitting the seeds into the shared dish pans—oh, well, I have quite a list of pictures I did not take while we were in China.

The banquet hosted by the Number Two Middle School that night was even grander than the ones the two previous days. I sat next to the chief administrator for the county. His personnel director was there, as was the party secretary. The head of the city educational bureau and the chief administrators for the host middle school were there. We ate in a bare cement room in the middle school and many of the guests were dressed casually, in walking shorts and white tee shirts, but the table was lavish. There were at least fifteen specialty food dishes, but the primary focus was on the toasts. The beverages were warm beer, warm Pepsi cola and warm Chinese 7-Up. Many of the toasts call for 'bottoms up' and the glasses are drained. I have wanted to count the number of toasts at a banquet, but I never think of it in time, but there must be dozens. Even when you only drink part of your glassful, someone is there to refill your glass, and to demonstrate generosity they usually keep pouring until your glass overflows.

The next morning it was our turn. Leona and I gave presentations on teaching methodology to about fifty English teachers from the various middle schools in the city. We were asked to give one hour "lectures," but we always involved our Chinese audiences in pairs, groups of fours, word games, T.P.R., and used a variety of other techniques to demonstrate that the lecture is the least effective method of teaching a foreign language. When we opened it up for questions, there were very few. Being all English teachers they were too shy to speak English in front of their colleagues for fear of making a grammatical error. Then when we adjourned, they all crowded around and asked questions. In addition to the usual grammar or technique questions we were surprised by the following, "When I try to use creative techniques in my class, my supervisor criticizes me and says, "Get Back to the Basics. What shall I do?"

Following the question/answer period our three students invited us to take a van ride in the countryside. Taoism was founded in the sixth century, B. C., by the philosopher Lao-Tse, and became one of the major philosophies in China. According to Taoism the Tao is *the path.* Whoever follows the path must be kind and free from pride. One of the early centers for Taoism, one of the places where it all began, was in a small village just two hours away. We said, "Let's go!"

After traveling over the dirt washboard road we arrived at the Temple of Celestial Beings which served as the home for the Taoist leader two thousand years ago. (Our students referred to him as the Taoist Pope.) We saw the living quarters for the Taoist Pope's family. We walked in the garden, and along a small lake where the Pope went fishing. The buildings and grounds showed neglect. The new government after Liberation in nineteen forty-nine has budgeted little money for the maintenance of a Taoist center which advocates a competing philosophy. The site was still impressive, but more for its historical significance. The Center was surrounded by a high wall that enclosed spacious grounds with lovely old trees. It was very hot and humid, but the shade and the breeze kept it comfortable. We had brought a picnic lunch. We spread a cloth on the ground. Kent's wife had made some *zhongzhis* (glutinous rice wrapped in bamboo leaves), a traditional food for Dragon Boat Festival. We also had boiled eggs, bread, bananas and warm soda pop.

The little village that surrounded the Taoist Temple grounds was where Green and Kent had spent their first few years teaching middle school before they were moved into the town schools. The village school is now boarded up and the village children have become boarding school children in Number Four Middle School in Gui Xi. The housing next to the Taoist Temple reminded me of the transient fruit pickers' camps in the San Joaquin Valley in California in the 1940's. When the weather is hot, the houses are hot, and everyone sits out in front, some preparing vegetables for dinner and some just shooting the breeze. Green and Kent asked our driver to stop. They went into some of the houses; they knew everybody from their teaching days. No one in China ever moves. We were not invited in. Green and Jean had not even invited us into their present homes in Gui Xi; they said they were too shabby.

On the way back to Gui Xi, we stopped at the Lu Li Hu River. Our students rented a boat. It was about five feet wide and forty feet long. The boat was ancient. It had ten little benches on each side. The benches were held in place by square nails about four inches long driven through the side of the boat. The boat was propelled by poling. A friendly young woman stood on the bow and held a long bamboo pole with a metal tip. An older man poled from the stern. They took us upstream for about forty-five minutes. When we reached deeper water the man switched to a large single oar. Our party, the three students and our driver, and Leona and I were the only passengers. It was hot and muggy. We still had our umbrellas for shade, and now we were happy to have them. Leona took off her shoes and hung her feet in the water. None of the Chinese students took off their plastic sandals or put their feet in the water.

The scenery was beautiful. The sharp hills on either side of the river resembled the limestone mountains in Guilin, the kind one sees in traditional Chinese paintings. Steep cliffs rose up on one side, four or five hundred feet high. In the higher portions of the cliffs were small caves where the ancients suspended their caskets. The moderns, however, have never determined how the caskets were raised that high. Way up high we could see caskets, or something, in a two of them. We passed by a very small village and watched a small boat lead a young water buffalo swimming across the river. The water was peaceful, the scenery was pretty, and the life all around us was so interesting. Our polers said if we paid them some money, they would tell the stories of the area. We told our students we would pay if they told the stories in English, which of course was a false hope. Apparently our students paid them something because they proceeded to talk. We passed a collection of two or three buildings backed up against the cliffs, and our guides said the Taoist Pope's mother used to live there, but she was always tormented by mosquitoes. The Pope's mother cast a spell on the mosquitoes, and to this day there are no mosquitoes there. Well, there weren't!

That evening the banquet was hosted by the municipal government. The food was lavish, the officials congenial, and the toasts never-ending. Turtle must be a popular food in that region. The only dish that was new to us was the chicken legs—that is, legs below the knees. They call them Phoenix Claws. Fortunately, when there are so many dishes, one doesn't feel obligated to eat everything.

After the banquet Jean said she and her family would visit us at the hotel. Her husband is the personnel director for the county. In China a personnel director is the one who assigns people to their life work and therefore carries considerable clout. They also had a six year old girl. They finally arrived about nine forty-five. Jean's husband had a meeting. In the middle of the meeting the chief administrator told him to go and said he could take his car and of course, the driver. We were impressed at his effort to come. Their little girl is really cute and lively. She has a cute smile and a twinkle in her eye. Leona gave her a Goldilocks pop-up book. Leona had also brought some of a frosted cake she had made from a cake mix in a care package from home and was able to serve our guests in style. Jean and her husband presented us with two large porcelain vases and a bag of fruit. They only stayed about twenty minutes. Jean's husband does not speak English, and lengthy conversations become very awkward.

Our train did not leave until noon, so we thought we had time for one more outing. Since it was Sunday the children were free to go with us. Our three students and one of their colleagues each had their one child. The six and seven year old girls were dressed in their festive best, pretty white lacy dresses, and Jean's daughter had bright rouge on her cheeks. The two men each had a ten year old son. We would go in two vans. Unfortunately the driver could not get one of them started and the other one had a flat tire. Eventually they finished patching the tire, and then we all pushed the other van to get it started.

We drove about forty minutes to an area similar to one of our state parks in California. There were low hills with interesting rock formations—the Chinese had identified several as "an old man," "a frog," "a lion," etc.—and lots of hiking trails. It was a beautiful setting, and more importantly to us, it had turned foggy and cool. The two girls tried to look pretty for about five minutes, and then ran all over and had a good time. Seeing how much the children enjoyed the outing, I asked Green how often he and his son were able to go on outings together. Green replied, "Perhaps once a year."

At the end of the hike the parents bought each of the children a treat, and everyone lined up for pictures. On the way back, three of the children rode in the back seat of my van, and they all promptly got car sick. I felt right at home.

We had our final luncheon—another gala event, with turtle, whole frogs, squid, pine nuts with pork, duck and chicken, and finally, in response to Leona's earlier request, some egg plant. Veggies are not very high on their list when they plan a banquet. We had enough toasts to last the year, and everyone went with us to the train station.

Jean's husband, the personnel director for the county, left work to come and see us off. He even carried a couple of our bags to the train; our bags had increased with gifts and extra fruit.

Jean had told her daughter to kiss "Granny" and "Grandpa" good-bye. As the train pulled in, I picked her up and she kissed me on the cheek. Jean said, "You have to kiss him on both cheeks so that he will have good luck!"

As the train pulled out of the station, we waved our arms until they felt as if they were going to fall off, and wondered what we could ever do for an encore.

Jangshu Goes International

On June tenth the Foreign Affairs Office provided a one-day trip for all of us foreign teachers in Nanchang. We would be bused to Jangshu, a small city about seventy kilometers due south of Nanchang, to attend a traditional Chinese Medicine festival. We had lived in China for almost a year at this point, but we were not able to anticipate what was going to happen.

We boarded our university bus at five-thirty a. m., and joined the other teachers in the Nanchang downtown square shortly thereafter. There were twenty-five American teachers and about fifteen Chinese staff; we would take two small buses. The seventy kilometers took two hours, and we were led by a police escort the entire way.

Even though it had rained almost every day, it was constantly hot. We had opened all of our windows in Nanchang on the tenth of May, and they had not been closed since that time. Now we were opening all of the bus windows, even at that early hour. The countryside was green and beautiful. The fields had all been cultivated and the rice planted. The water buffalo had completed their work and were now "on vacation," but they still had to eat. About every hundred yards a water buffalo was grazing on weeds next to a rice paddy. Each one was tended by a boy or an old man. The hundred yard intervals resulted from each family farming two to two and a half acres and no peasant owns more than one water buffalo.

Jangshu had only been open to foreigners for one year. After the city was opened, I am not sure any foreigners wanted to go there. During the day we were there, we certainly did not see any.

As our two buses entered the city, hundreds of people lined the streets, apparently waiting for us. As we neared the hotel where we would eat our meals, a children's drum and bugle corps in full uniform sounded their greeting. Before we had time to react to this public welcome, we were taken to the city stadium. As we stepped down from our buses, we were greeted by photographers, with still cameras and with television cameras, taking our pictures as we entered the stadium. We were escorted into privileged seats in the stadium, and the photographers continued to take our picture as we found our seats. This was the first International Traditional Chinese Festival. Apparently they had been short of foreigners and had imported our group of twenty-five American teachers so they could declare their festival international. We all thought we would probably appear on all of their public relations news clips and future brochures advertising the event for next year.

The stadium field was filled with colorful performing groups: little girls with crepe paper rainbows that they moved in rhythm over their heads, slightly larger girls with pink netting that they waved in unison, still larger girls with bouquets of artificial flowers, young men in gyrating dragons, a marching band, an adult parade group carrying flags, men on stilts dressed in medieval dress. The display reminded us of the Asian Games festivities we had seen on Chinese television. Photographers continued to photograph the audience. In our V. I. P. seating section we found plastic water bottles under our seats, presented as gifts, and a bottle of Chinese seven-up for our enjoyment.

The other sections of the stadium were full, and another five thousand people stood around the edge of the field. In fact, the stadium was already full when we arrived, and as soon as we were seated, the festivities began.

Five hundred pigeons were released and fluttered over the stadium. Hundreds of firecrackers helped set the festive tone. They raised two flags, one was the flag of the Peoples' Republic of China. The other flag was "The International Traditional Chinese Medicine Festival." Over the public address system one of our teachers was introduced. She was the one who was teaching at the Traditional Chinese

Medicine college in Nanchang. She gave a brief welcome and thank you in English. Several Chinese officials gave brief welcomes in Chinese. Then everyone in the center of the stadium formed into a parade and marched past us, doing their dancing, gyrating, music playing, and stilt walking. The entire performance was over within thirty minutes and we were back on our buses. We were scheduled to tour the local traditional Chinese medicine factory. As we drove through town, we caught up with the parade, and the parade crowd. Our buses were in the middle of thousands of people. The crowd stretched from our bus, across the sidewalks to the buildings. The crowd filled intersections and side streets. People were standing close together, waiting, and watching. I have never seen so many people in one spot. But it was a happy crowd in a festive mood, and they gave the foreigners an enthusiastic welcome. People were waving from upper story windows and roof tops. People just outside the bus windows smiled and waved. Parents held up small children so they could see the foreigners. I took pictures of the people looking at the people looking. . .

After touring the traditional Chinese medicine factory, we went to a winery. We were again welcomed with firecrackers and a thirteen-man dragon dance group. As we walked through the winery, I kept looking for grapes. There was a strong odor, but it was too strong for wine. I soon learned that their beverage was made from rice. They produced two basic varieties, one "wine" had an alcoholic content of thirty-six percent, and the other "wine" had an alcoholic content of fifty-two percent.

We returned to the hotel for a banquet meal. There were no speeches and no toasts, but every bite was recorded for possible use on local television.

After lunch we were taken out of town to see their local attraction. As soon as we left the town, we also left the crowds and the public eye. Our tour became routine. After riding on the bus for about thirty minutes we came to a fork in the road. There was a large road sign: "The Scenic

Spot," with a directional arrow. The scenic spot turned out to be a Taoist Temple.

We returned to the hotel for an excellent supper, but without the television crews. The police again escorted us back to Nanchang.

How's Your Grammar?

One of our Chinese colleagues in the Training Center at the Jiangxi Teachers University was Gan Lin. He was 24, and therefore was called *Xiao* Gan, meaning young Gan. Although he did have some administrative duties, his entire teaching assignment was four hours of Intensive Reading, two two-hour classes each week. Intensive Reading is appropriately named, one week of four class hours on each lesson, a simplified story four or five pages long. Intensive Reading is considered to be so important in preparation for the qualifying examinations, universities that do have some foreign teachers generally reserve this course for one of the Chinese staff. I was assigned a class in second year Intensive Reading during the middle of the spring semester in Nanjing in 1986 when the Chinese instructor became ill and was hospitalized. In Nanjing the course was one hour per day, five days a week. I found it difficult to spend five hours on so few pages. My students helped by asking questions like, "What does this word modify? What is the antecedent for that word?" I tried to re-direct their focus from structure to meaning by teaching outlining and summarizing.

Xiao Gan told me one day that he had told his father that he was working with two foreign teachers that year, and his father's response was, "Well, where are they?" Xiao Gan said that his father lived about an hour's drive from Nanchang, and sometime he would arrange a car to take us there for a visit. I said that we could go by bus, but Xiao Gan's father was a cadre (an official), and Xiao Gan felt it was important that we travel by car.

Mr. Gan had been vice president of a State Farm which had a population of 17,000. In January he had been named manager of a pharmaceutical factory located on the State Farm. The factory had 600 employees.

On Thursday, May 23, Xiao Gan said, "On Sunday we will go and visit my father. I have arranged for a car." (He never mentioned his mother.) The car arrived about 9:15 that Sunday morning and we had a very pleasant ride out through the country. The last nine miles, however, we rode through road construction that was more interesting than pleasant, particularly when we reached a muddy stretch about 50 feet long. The driver asked us all to get out and walk a rice paddy levee around the bad stretch, and then he slithered through and picked us up on the far side.

During the trip Xiao Gan had a chance to tell us more about the State Farm. His father's pharmaceutical factory produced mostly traditional Chinese medicine. There were two other pharmaceutical factories, a video tape factory, a silk factory, two wineries, and a variety of agricultural products. The crops included rice, pork, wine grapes, plums, peaches, and mulberry trees for the silk worms.

The headquarters of the State Farm was a village of about 10,000. As we entered the village Xiao Gan asked if it would be o. k. if we visited his middle school English teacher. We said that would be fine. Our car drove straight to the middle school. We were unconcerned; most teachers live on campus. As we drove through the main gate of the school, Xiao Gan said, "The students will be excited to see you; they are waiting for you." This was on a Sunday morning. He had said nothing about our meeting with students.

We walked across the campus of the school. It included about 2000 students grades 7-12. We went to some apartment houses on the far side of the soccer field, and to Xiao Gan's former English teacher's home. We were served tea and fruit. After the preliminary greetings, I asked him what course he was teaching. He said, "Senior middle, grade 3 English." (All middle school English in China is taught as Intensive Reading, and they all use the same book. He was teaching the grade equivalent of grade twelve in the U.S.) We were using this same material in the Training Center in order to help our middle school teachers improve their methodology, so I asked, "What book are you using?" He said, "Senior middle, grade 2 English." Since his students had already had that book the previous year, and being Intensive Reading, practically memorized it, I asked, "Why are you repeating last year's book?" He said, "The College Entrance Examination does not include Book 3."

We then went to the main classroom building. We walked past an open classroom door and saw a classroom of fifty or sixty students waiting for us. They all waved, but we walked on by. We were taken to the faculty lounge where four other teachers were waiting for us. We were served tea and began introducing ourselves. One teacher had taught 5 years, another 8, and the department chairperson 10 years. After we talked a while, the department chairperson took out a paper and formally read the following, "Could you tell us please, the difference between *f i r m* and *f i r m l y*, when *firm* is used as an adverb?"

We were aghast. These English teachers had seldom talked with a native speaker of English; some may never have had the opportunity. They had all been teaching English for several years. They obviously had more advance notice of our meeting than we did. This was their big chance to talk to us, and this was the important question they had prepared in advance- the Westerner just cannot imagine the focus Chinese teachers and their students place on grammar.

We were taken into the classroom full of students, fifty or sixty twelfth graders sitting close together, but with bright eyes and smiling faces. They all applauded as we entered. I wondered on that Sunday morning how long they had been waiting for us. We each gave a short presentation. Foreign teachers in China are referred to as "foreign experts," but we felt that if we had had any advance warning at all we could surely have done a better job.

After our presentations the students were given time to ask questions. One of the questions by a female student, perhaps 17 years old, was, "Can we be friends?" Leona answered, "Of course." The student continued, "Can I have my picture taken with you?" Leona suggested we have our pictures taken with all of the students, so we sat down on one side of the room and then the other since they were using our camera and we did not have a wide angle lens.

We were then taken to the best restaurant in town where Mr. Gan joined us. We were served two dishes offish, frogs, pork and potatoes, garlic stems, Phoenix claws, eel, quail eggs, mushroom soup, and for beverage, Pepsi and Chinese beer.

Following lunch we were taken to Xiao Gan's parents' home. When we arrived at the home, we walked down a 6 foot path with a solid brick wall on both sides, for about 100 feet to their front door. The front of their home was three rooms, the kitchen, Mr. Gan's office and the bathroom including a toilet and a shower, and the laundry room. Then we walked through a courtyard and entered the living room. There were two bedrooms on one side and one on the other. As we were walking in, Xiao Gan confided with me, "It is nice to be a cadre." The living room was small with a comfortable couch on one side and a large refrigerator on the other. (In China it is not unusual to have the refrigerator, frequently the best appliance in the home, in the living room.)

Xiao Gan introduced us to his girl friend. She was living with his parents, and they planned on getting married "soon." She was an accountant in the video tape factory, and was one year older than Xiao Gan. I noticed a pile of rather rough soft wood lumber stacked in Xiao Gan's bedroom (he only lives there during holiday periods now.) Xiao Gan explained that the lumber was for their furniture when they get married, and he showed us scale sketches of a bed, a wardrobe, and a dresser.

We then visited Mr. Gan's factory. Since it was Sunday, the factory was closed. There were some cleaning and maintenance crews working, but the buildings were locked. We walked around and looked through the windows. The families of the 600 employees live in apartment houses on the factory grounds. We visited Mr. Gan's secretary, a man, who lived in one of the apartments. Before he was Mr. Gan's secretary, he had been Xiao Gan's junior high Chinese teacher. He had three lovely teen aged daughters. The oldest daughter had failed the university entrance examinations the previous year, and now she worked in one of the factories at the State Farm where her mother also worked. The other two daughters were still in middle school. While we were drinking our tea, one of the girls handed me an orange that she had just peeled for me. I was most impressed. I am not used to having teen agers peel oranges for me. When we were ready to leave, our host, the secretary, presented us with a gift, six porcelain tri-color horses. We were amazed. We had never even met this man before, and yet he was giving us a lovely gift.

We returned to the family home for a "simple" supper. Mr. Gan's secretary joined us for the meal, as did our driver, and Xiao Gan's brother, and parents. I looked at the table setting. At each place there was a shot glass and a rice bowl. I would ignore the shot glass, but I felt relieved that there was a rice bowl. At Chinese dinners, the serving dishes are placed in the middle of the table and everyone eats directly from these community dishes with chop sticks. When one has a plate (or in this case a rice bowl) one can use it as a landing place or half-way stop, particularly for the more slippery bites. Without any plate at all, eating with chop sticks without dropping anything becomes a real challenge.

We all sat down at the table and Mr. Gan filled each of the shot glasses with some kind of spirits, and then to my dismay, Xiao Gan filled all of the rice bowls with Pepsi Cola. We lost our "landing place," During the course of the dinner, however, there must have been 15 or 20 toasts. Leona and I were glad we had the Pepsi Cola.

The dinner was fun. There was loud talking, good camaraderie with all of the toasts, and gracious serving of tasty, home cooked food. The dinner included six dishes plus *jiaozis*.

Following dinner, as part of our farewells, Mr. and Mrs. Gan gave us a set of 4 porcelain plates, rice bowls and porcelain spoons. Xiao Gan gave us a porcelain statue of a female Buddha who held a bottle that slowly dripped water into a dragon's mouth, and his brother gave me some Chinese stamps. We felt very honored by their gracious hospitality.

Welcome Stranger

Delia, a Chinese teacher, taught a community English class three nights a week. In order to expose the students to a native English speaker, she invited me to lecture to them for one hour each week. In order to repay me for my contribution, she asked if we would like to visit Inner Mongolia. Her husband was going to graduate school in Hoh Hot, the capital of Inner Mongolia, and he would serve as our guide. Leona and I were planning to visit Beijing at the end of the school year, and Hoh Hot is just an overnight train ride north west of Beijing. I told Delia that we would love to go. When I gave Delia the dates when we would be available, she said that her husband would have already left, but that he would ask a friend to show us around.

Our train arrived in Hoh Hot at about seven-thirty in the morning. On the platform we were immediately approached by a young woman, "Trip to the Grasslands? Do you want to take a grasslands tour?" We said, "No thank you," but she was quite persistent, so we had to say no several times. Then we spied a young man holding a small sign saying, "DAMERON," and we introduced ourselves to Shang who was Delia's husband's friend.

Shang had been unable to get the inexpensive room at the university guest house, but with his help, we checked into the expensive tourist hotel for one night, intending to transfer to the university quarters on the following day. The hotel was lovely, the day was lovely, and we truly felt we were on vacation. Nanchang, where we had been teaching, had had a terrible climate with the humidity high enough to grow mold on our clothes in the closet. But Hoh Hot is in western China where the summers are dry and the humidity is low like it is at home in California.

After spending a sleepless night on the train Leona wanted to rest, but I was restless and went for a walk. I went several blocks and then turned up the main street. I was disappointed. The city was more developed than Nanchang; it did not have the swarms of free market vendors and local color I expected. I decided to re-trace my steps and return to the hotel.

Suddenly I heard the familiar, "Hello." That is the common greeting given by a Chinese person to an English speaking foreigner, and frequently is the extent of their English vocabulary. I turned. The greeting had come from three or four young men sitting out in front of a little shop. I walked back to where they were and began talking to them, although our conversation was as limited as my Chinese vocabulary. After a few minutes the proprietor, who was listening to our conversation, brought me a small stool to sit on, and after I sat down, he too, joined in the conversation. Several others gathered around, some speaking Chinese, most just listening. A young woman joined in; she spoke English. She was an attorney, and her husband was in the import/export business. She said her husband had visited our west coast several times, particularly Seattle, Washington. The proprietor gave me a popsicle. As I sat on that stool, eating a popsicle, with about ten people gathered around listening, I continued to talk with the attorney. She was the only one who spoke English. Then the proprietor interrupted. He wanted me to take a picture of him standing in front of his shop. I stepped back and began adjusting my camera. He said to make sure the picture included the name of his shop—the Chinese characters were painted just above the doorway. I handed my camera to one of the young men. I lined up with the proprietor, the attorney, and two others on a row of chairs in front of the shop, and everyone else took their places behind us. The picture was taken. I got the address from the attorney and two months later I mailed them a delightful five by seven picture from California as a reminder of that delightful experience one afternoon in Hoh Hot, Inner Mongolia.

I received in reply a delightful response:

> Many thanks for your letter and the picture. I am very sorry I am so late to answer you.
>
> I appreciated meeting you very much, as I have many friends in China, but I haven't any friends from foreign country until I meet you in Huh Hot City.
>
> I have one boy and one daughter. In China two children means very very happy as our government allow every young couple only have one child. . .
>
> In your letter I found you like China and think our Huh Hot City is very beautiful. There are many places you did not go to, so if you want to go to our city next time, I'll lead you. If you come to Huh Hot City next time, pls let me know, and my tel. no. is_____(home). I am waiting to meet you next time. I think we must have a wonderful time in Huh Hot City.

Sincerely yours,
Xu Qing Mei

The next morning while exploring in the hotel we found the Tourism Office. It was operated by the government and offered trips to the Grasslands, two days for one hundred sixty yuan, or one day for ninety to one hundred five yuan, depending on how many were in the party. On the overnight trip guests would sleep in a Mongolian yurt. We told Shang about the government tours and told him the prices.

Shang said, "We can rent our own car and go much cheaper."

We asked, "How much cheaper?"

He said that our taxi driver would take us on a one day trip to a Mongolian village out in the grasslands for sixty yuan. We said that we would think about that and let him know. Meanwhile we had to move our things to the university guest house.

During the next few days Shang and his sister showed us the scenic spots in and around Hoh Hot City. Shang's sister had just graduated from a language school in Beijing and spoke very good English. We rented bicycles and rode through the old section of the city with its narrow alleys and free market sidewalk vendors. We visited an ancient Llama Buddhist center, Dazhao Temple, built during the fifteenth century, and the Five Pagoda Temple, built in seventeen thirty-three. We rode a public bus out to the tomb of Wang Zhao Jun who was a Chinese princess who helped preserve the peace by marrying a rival Hun prince in 33 B. C.

Since the Chinese constitution was revised in nineteen seventy-nine, churches and places of worship have been allowed to re-open. In Hoh Hot City we visited a modern Moslem mosque on Friday afternoon, right after prayer time, and on Sunday morning attended a worship service at a Christian church.

We decided to rent a car for a trip to the Grasslands. The government Tourist Bureau trip would be better organized and perhaps more informative, but on a private trip we could take Shang and his sister. We felt we owed them that much.

The taxi arrived, or rather the taxi driver arrived, on Monday morning at seven-thirty. He had removed all taxi identification from his car. Shang came into the lobby. "The driver has said, 'Ninety yuan.'" We were startled. We thought the price had already been settled. Shang said, "He will drive us to Xilamuren. It is more than eighty-five kilometers." I said that we would cancel the trip. Ninety yuan was too much. Shang talked to the driver. Shang returned and reported, "The driver will take you to the Grasslands for seventy-five yuan." We had bread, canned meat, a dozen boiled eggs, and several bottles of soda pop already purchased.

"O. K., Let's go."

As we started to get into the car, however, we were troubled by Shang's remark, "If anyone asks, you are foreign experts and we are just friends of yours."

We headed north. It was a beautiful day. Unlike south China, the humidity was low and the sky was blue. After a few miles we entered the Daqing Mountains, and climbed to the summit, three or four thousand feet high. There were occasional trees along the stream beds, but generally there was only grass. From the summit we looked out across the plains; there were the grasslands. We continued along a two laned paved highway. We saw small herds of sheep and grazing horses. Small clusters of mud brick houses were connected by rock wall fences.

We arrived at Xilamuren about ten-thirty. It was a sleepy little village. There was only one main street with a few shops. A half-dozen people were walking around. There was a small collection of homes. Everything was dusty and quiet. At the edge of town there was a collection of Mongolian yurts, obviously erected for tourists.

We took pictures of the yurts, and then asked if we could go inside one for a closer look. Shang asked permission. The answer was, "No, they are reserved for the government tours." It took us about thirty minutes to check out all the sights in town, a Llama Buddhist temple, a few horses grazing near-by, and to take a picture of the sweeping grasslands beyond. We were very disappointed. The village was not Mongolian; the buildings and the people were all Chinese, and the yurts were a government monopoly.

"Well, let's eat our lunch."

We sat on the raised sidewalk next to a building. I cut open the bread rolls and opened the can of meat and began slicing it for sandwiches. We balanced fruit, boiled eggs, and soda pop on our laps.

At that moment a government official came out of the tourism office and said, "You will have to leave. You are not part of a government tour."

We said, "O. K., we will eat over there, under those trees."

The official said, "No, you may not stay anywhere in this village."

Leona and I were furious. We were not angry at the official because we knew we could not fight city hall. No, we were angry at our driver. He talked us into the trip so he could get his fare, but he must have known that we would not be welcome. Why else would he have removed his taxi identification. We closed up our sandwiches, picked up our eggs and fruit and soda, got back in the car and left town. We were not used to being run out of town. We felt like we were in an old western movie.

About ten miles up the road our driver turned off into a grain field onto a one lane dirt road. We found a row of poplar trees, all topped at about eight feet. They were bushy and provided minimal shade. We sat down in the dirt between rows of stunted grain. It was hot and dry. We huddled next to the poplar trees for shade. I handed each person a bread roll and a slice of meat. Sitting on the ground, we peeled our boiled eggs, ate our bananas, and washed it all down with warm soda pop. Everything was so ridiculous; I took a picture of the group. After lunch we headed back toward Hoh Hot City.

On one of the slopes of the Daqing Mountains we stopped and got out. Shang and I began walking up the slope. We walked through lush grass and beautiful wild flowers a foot deep. On the top of the hill we could see miles and miles of grasslands. This had been the home of Genghis Khan and his Mongol hordes in the twelfth century. Genghis Khan's grandson, Kublai Khan, was the emperor of all of China when Marco Polo came there in 1215.

Apparently he received a better welcome by the government officials than we did.

Chapter V

Let's Celebrate

"Fourth of July" in China

China's "Fourth of July" or Independence Day is October first, the day Liberation was proclaimed by Chairman Mao Tse Tung in Tiananmen Square in 1949. National Day is China's second most important holiday, and prompts parades, parties and family gatherings.

This year October first fell on a Monday, just two days before Mid-autumn Festival which is determined by the Chinese lunar calendar. The university extended the usual two-day vacation for National Day to three days to include the second holiday as well.

Our students had all left homes and families to come to the university for a year of study, and they would all take this opportunity to go home. In their classroom essays, as noted in Chapter Three, they had written about extended family gatherings and holiday dinners. They had told of gifts of moon cakes and fruit, or new shoes for a child, a shirt for a husband and wine for a father. Some of our students would travel three or four hours by bus to near-by communities; others would travel ten to fifteen hours by train and bus to their more remote villages.

On Friday preceding National Day the Training Center Director came to my classroom and said, "We will come to your apartment on Saturday evening for dinner. We will come at six o'clock. We will bring some Chinese food, and you prepare some American food." I responded simply with, "O. K."

The next day we received additional information, "They will go to your apartment at three o'clock and make jiaozis (Chinese dumplings)."

"O. K."

Leona and I decided we would bring fried potatoes and apple sauce. Rice is the staple food, but potatoes are generally available in the vegetable market. We borrowed a hot plate from an American colleague, set it on our tiled bathroom floor, and I fried the potatoes. We had found ketchup in the local department store. The apple sauce was easy because Leona had brought cinnamon from the United States; we had not been able to find any in China. Karen, an American colleague, made pop corn.

Director Xu and Mrs. Zhang, a clerk, arrived promptly at three o'clock. They brought a box of loose rice flour, a bowl of pre-mixed meat/vegetable filling for the jiaozis, and several bunches of green onions. We washed off the top of our study desk, sprinkled it with flour, and Mrs. Zhang and Leona rolled out the dough. Director Xu had me chop the green onions; he had brought a large meat cleaver for that purpose. Then we started making the jiaozis. We rolled out the dough into three-inch-round discs, with chop sticks we dropped a "spoonful" of meat/vegetable filling, then folded and crimped the edges. Everyone had his/her own style. Leona and I tried our luck. Two Chinese teachers joined in. The lady house-manager had to demonstrate her skill. Director Xu and Mrs. Zhang demonstrated their artistry. In about two hours we had rolled, stuffed, and squeezed one hundred eighty jiaozis. Then everyone went home to get their food contributions for the pot luck.

There were nine of us at the potluck banquet, six Chinese, Karen, another American teaching in the Training Center, and Leona and me. The food was great. We shared loud talking and laughter, compliments on each others' dishes, and presented many toasts. When we finished there was lots of food left over, but our fried potatoes were gone.

The pot luck ended abruptly at seven-twenty because we had been invited to Karen's sophomore class party scheduled for seven-thirty. When we arrived her classroom had been decorated with crepe paper streamers, and a tape player was playing popular Chinese music. Chairs lined the walls, leaving the center of the classroom open. We were served a can of Lady cola, spicy hot candied peanuts, millet crisp crust (corn chips) and Mid-autumn Festival moon cakes.

After formal introductions, the entertainment began. With minimal encouragement Chinese like to perform, and even those with little talent will stand and sing, sometimes stopping half way through a song with "That's all I know." To present some organization to the performances a crepe paper flower was passed around the room from hand to hand. The leader was beating on a tom-tom type drum. Whoever was caught with the flower when the drum sound stopped, was obligated to sing a song or give some performance. There were several renditions of "Edelweiss." Two girls donned simple costumes and presented a dance. Three young men sang "500 Miles." An ex-professional singer sang a song from a Beijing opera. We were most impressed when three young women in costume performed a mock western wedding. When it was my turn I led the group on a Lion Hunt, which is a children's story in which walking, running, jumping, or crossing a bridge is indicated by patting one's legs or chest at different speeds.

Then the dancing began. Most of the songs were waltzes. Three or four boys were very good, but many of the students and Leona and I did not attempt any of the waltzes. Eventually they played a song we could dance to, and we each accepted student invitations to dance. I only danced one dance. My dance partner, a twenty year old university sophomore, said she did not have the opportunity to go to many dances. She was very shy, but was obviously enjoying this chance to dance.

The Chinese are very patriotic. As Leona and I rode bicycles to church on Sunday morning, National Day weekend, we rode past the downtown square. It was filled with people, thousands of people, with flags and banners waving everywhere. There were military groups, organized school classes, and common citizens. One group of girls was singing a patriotic song over loud speakers. There was a festive air. As we turned down a side street we passed a military unit marching and calling out their cadence in unison. Their voices reverberated in the narrow street. When we reached the Christian church, however, we found it was full as usual.

That evening all of the foreign teachers from throughout the city were invited to a banquet sponsored by the provincial government. There was a long buffet table artistically decorated and filled with fancy dishes. The dinner was hosted by the vice-governor. Guests sat at round tables in groups of eight, and the vice-governor went to each table to greet us individually. He was accompanied by his aides and a television crew. After the banquet we moved to the hotel ballroom. The entertainment included singing, a juggling act, and a young woman performing on a unicycle. Following the entertainment the evening was concluded with dancing.

In November, as part of the American culture class, I told the story of Thanksgiving, the Pilgrims celebrating their first Thanksgiving with three days of feasting and games with their Indian friends, and the contemporary celebration with family and the traditional dinner. I asked my students if at some point during the year, they reflected on their family, their crop harvest, and their good fortune and gave thanks. One student responded, "No, we are usually too busy."

When one is living in a foreign culture where the people do not celebrate one's customary holidays, you become lonely and reflective at holiday time. In November, 1990, I shared these feelings with friends at home in the following article.

Be Thankful[1]

At this time of year when we reflect on our many blessings, one that heads most of our lists is our family. Being sixteen time zones away from our children and grandchildren and living on letters and snap shots, remind us how precious our family is. We also appreciate our homes. Our homes in Galt and Lodi are spacious, warm, and filled with modern conveniences including running water, both hot and cold, stoves with ovens, modern bathrooms, and carpeting. Something we tend to overlook, however, is the freedom to live where we want. If we do not like our house or apartment, we can move. We have also tended to overlook our automobiles and the independence and pleasure they provide.

In the past we have not recognized the importance of a dependable and confidential mail service, an efficient telephone system, grocery stores with sanitary meat departments, and the November elections.

Our lives in China contrast sharply with our lives back home. Here we cannot drink the tap water and have hot water only on occasion. We eat rice three times a day, have very little meat, and the only milk we get is powdered. We do our shopping and run our errands by bicycle. Our packages are inspected at the post office before we can seal them and many of our letters are opened as well. We teach in unheated classrooms and feel blessed when all the lights work. There is no custodian service. But when we invite students to our apartment they are impressed with its spaciousness and when they see our terrible carpeting, they ask if they should take their shoes off. Our life in China, compared to that of our Chinese students, is again something to be thankful for.

Our students are thirty-five to forty-five years old. They have been teaching English at the middle school level in small villages and towns for many years. Since they never had the opportunity to go to a college or be taught by a

---

1 *The Lodi News Sentinel*, Nov. 17, 1990, p. 4 .

native English speaking teacher, oral English is still very difficult for them. In order to improve themselves, however, they have left homes and families for one year to come to the University where they are living seven to a room.

Our students are very homesick for their homes and families even though by our standards their homes are pretty basic. Many of their homes lack any running water at all. Their kitchens are very minimal, and the neighborhood toilet is down the alley somewhere. One student said his home is fifty kilometers from the larger town. He teaches in a junior high school and his son attends the same school, but the son will have to move into town when he is ready for senior high school.

In their essays, however, the students comment on how much better things are than before "Liberation" in 1949:

> Before Liberation my hometown was a sad and dirty little town. Along the entire street one could see rubbish, rats, and other waste matter. The litter gave off a terrible smell. Most people were very poor. Only a few families were rich. Many had no work and their children often went hungry.
>
> Everything has changed now. The people have got rid of the mud and dirt. They have put up schools, theaters, shops, and hotels, and a big park. Every morning the dustmen are collecting the rubbish. Now the whole street is not only uniform but also is clean. Our lives are getting better and better too. I love my hometown and love its people too. -Zhan Guang Xi

Finding the Christmas Spirit in China

We were standing at the bicycle parking lot entrance. The lot was full and the attendant was waiting for someone to leave before she would let us park. We watched the mass of shoppers jostling their way into the department store. It was the Sunday after Thanksgiving with only four weeks left to shop for Christmas. Finally we were able to park, and we too jockeyed our way into the store. We were looking for a gift for our daughter, but there were so many shoppers, we could not get close to the counter. From a distance we determined that this store did not have what we wanted so we went back to the parking lot, got on our bicycles, and headed for another store. But this was China, and in spite of the mobs of people in every store, we were the only ones who were Christmas shopping.

In the streets crowded with bicycles and carts, accentuated by honking horns and tinkling bicycle bells, on the sidewalks narrowed by free market vendors displaying their wares of tea eggs, winter coats, cheap jewelry, and plastic utensils, and in the department stores filled with the noise of bustling shoppers instead of recorded Christmas carols, how does one find the spirit of Christmas?

In order to mail a Christmas package home we needed to make a cloth bag, a postal requirement in China. "Say, we can go to one of those 'pedal pushers' on the street, the women who set up their sewing machines and make clothes to order." I hurried down the busy alley lined by free market vendors until I came to a tailor shop no more than five feet wide. A young man was working at an ironing board, and a young woman sat at a sewing machine beyond him. She quickly understood my request, rapidly stitched up the muslin into a bag and handed it to me.

"How much does it cost?"

She waved me away and said, "No charge," in Chinese. I laid a few small bills on the table; she picked them up and gave them back to me with a smile. Christmas spirit? I am afraid she did not know what Christmas spirit is.

In addition to teaching our middle school teachers English and teaching methodology, we were also expected to teach them about American culture. What better way to understand Christmas than by having a Christmas party, we thought. In typical American fashion we set up several committees. We asked the Training Center to provide us with a Christmas tree. They readily agreed; then asked,

"What does a Christmas tree look like?" Chinese stores sell colored lights, but no Christmas decorations. The decorations committee used red and green paper and made paper chains. We strung some dried red berries that resembled cranberries. We used foil from a chocolate bar to cover a cardboard star for the top of the tree. The tree tip was too limber, so one of our students re-enforced it with a chop stick. We had a reindeer picture in a children's coloring book. An art student painted a poster size Rudolph.

The music committee practiced "Santa Claus Is Coming to Town" and "Silver Bells" on the *erhu*, a two stringed violin, and a flute.

We had a little problem with the refreshments committee. When asked what was customary food at a party one said, "We usually just sit around and talk and eat water melon seeds." They did suggest oranges and Leona and I bought ten *jin* (about ten pounds.) Leona also had the women on the committee help her make Christmas cookies. We had no cookie cutters, so the stars and bells were custom made.

We told our students the Bible story of the birth of Jesus including the shepherds and the Wise Men. We explained that the gifts of the Wise Men established the basis for our gift giving today and had each student purchase and wrap an inexpensive gift and label it "man" or "woman." The thrust of the party had to remain secular, however, and the entertainment committee presented a skit on Rudolph the Red Nosed Reindeer. Leona's class sang, "Santa Claus Is Coming to Town." The entertainment also included "Edelweiss," of course, and one student did Tai Qi, a beautiful Chinese exercise routine.

Chinese Christians Celebrate Christmas

In our first year in China, in 1985/86, we attended St. Paul's Church in Nanjing. One Sunday morning while the congregation was filing out after the service, the choir gathered down in the front pews around the piano and began practicing. What caught our attention, however, was that they were singing Christmas carols. We could not resist going down front and listening. The choir director was one of the pastors, and when he saw how interested we were, asked, "Would you care to join us?"

We enthusiastically said, "Yes."

Choir practice was on Friday night. We rode our bicycles two miles on rough and dimly lit streets. It was December and the church was unheated. When we received our music there were no notes; Chinese music is written in sol fa, i. e. numbers one to seven for do, re, mi...and Chinese characters. Someone re-wrote the characters into Roman letters so we could pronounce the Chinese. The Christmas music was selections from Handel's Messiah. We did not sing the Sunday anthems. The Chinese was too difficult for us to learn a new song each week. The women in the choir were mostly young factory workers with pure strong voices. Many of the men were middle aged, and one was a dentist and another was a professor at Nanjing University. The Chinese choir members came to practice a half hour early for Bible study. We practiced with the choir for six weeks.

On Christmas Sunday St. Paul's Church was packed. People filled the aisles, the entry, the steps, and the crowd extended out into the courtyard. I wore long underwear, sweater and a warm jacket under my choir robe. I took off my stocking cap and gloves; like everyone else we had come to church on our bicycles and the church was unheated. The piano began. We lighted our candles and began our processional, singing Silent Night, in Chinese, of course. The service was inspirational and the choir's performance was beautiful.

Following the ninety minute worship service, there was a Christmas pageant, complete with Mary and Joseph, the babe in a manger, the shepherds and the Wise Men. The choir members were the actors. They had memorized their parts and were in full costume. The Wise Men and shepherds were men, but Mary and Joseph were both played by women. The shepherds wore real sheep skins.

On Christmas Day our choir sang at Mochou Street Church, and the uplifting experience was repeated. It seemed so incongruous to us, however, to have the church so jammed with enthusiastic worshippers while back at the university, classes were conducted as usual.

Chinese Christians Celebrate Easter

Six weeks before Easter Leona and I re-joined the choir. We again rode bicycles two miles every Friday night to an unheated church. They again re-wrote the Chinese into Roman letters, and we worked hard to learn the special music. We would sing at St. Paul's Church for the Good Friday service and at the Mochou Street Church on Easter Sunday morning.

On Thursday afternoon, the day before Good Friday, there was a knock on our door. It was the pastor/choir director. After the usual preliminaries he said, "This is Passion Week; I have bad news for you. I was unable to get permission for you to sing with us tomorrow."

We could not believe our ears. After going to choir practice for six weeks—memorizing the music—emotionally we were ready to sing. We were crushed. Then the pastor unrolled a Chinese scroll and presented it to us. Printed in Chinese characters was the Scripture reading, Matthew 20:28, "The son of man came not to be served, but to serve."

After the pastor left, we still felt miserable. Our first reaction was—we just wouldn't go to the service. After we thought about that for a while, we decided, "Well, we'd go, but we'd sit way in the back."

In spite of the crowds at the church the next day, the pastor found us after the service—sitting way back in the far corner of the church.

We told him, honestly, "The choir sounded lovely."

He responded, "But not as lovely, as if you could have sung with us."

The Christian Church in China

We arrived at the Nanchang Union Church at 8:15, a full fifteen minutes before the Sunday morning 8:30 service. It was World Communion Sunday, the first Sunday in October in 1990. We wheeled our bicycles past the hundreds of others parked along the sidewalk, into the courtyard, and squeezed them in among dozens of other parked bicycles. We folded up our plastic raincoats, took our Bible and Chinese hymn book from our bicycle baskets, and went up the steps.

We were met by an elderly Chinese woman, under five feet tall, wearing a tag pinned to her coat designating her as an usher. The church was already full. Many of the congregation had arrived at least 45 minutes early, and they were practicing the hymns. (We presumed they had to learn the hymns because the church had been closed for so many years in China.) One of the young assistant pastors led them phrase by phrase and line by line through the hymns that would be sung in the service that day. We turned sideways in order to squeeze through the crowd standing in the entry and followed the usher about halfway down the aisle to the seats she had saved for us. Knowing that she was saving seats for us every Sunday heightened our sense of commitment to attend regularly. The thought of having two seats remaining empty while Chinese worshippers were standing in the aisle and crowding all the entryways would have troubled us—particularly since many of them would know whose seats they were.

The Nanchang Union Church is the only open Protestant church in Nanchang, a city of more than one million people. Before Liberation there were ten Protestant churches (four were Methodist) with a membership of about 100 in each church. Today there is one church, (the

Chinese Christian Church is non-denominational) with a membership of about 3000. The church is supplemented by numerous house churches (some said there were 25 or 30 in Nanchang).

The elements of the worship service were familiar: Call to Worship, Scripture reading, prayer, anthem by the choir, and three hymns by the congregation. About two/thirds of the hymns were familiar. Some of the other hymns had been written by Chinese composers. The songs in our hymn book were printed in Chinese characters. As we had learned in our Nanjing choir experience there were no musical notes. The Chinese people use the Sol fa method (as in do re mi fa sol la ti do), and the notes are portrayed by the numbers one to seven. (A popular song in China is "Doe's a deer, a female deer," from *Sound of Music* because it is based on do, re, mi.)

I indicated that the church was full. The pews provided seating for about six hundred people. Another hundred worshippers stood in the aisles or sat on the cement floor on small round grass woven mats. Outside the windows on our side about 150 people sat on benches under a makeshift fiber glass roof, and on the other side of the church more people stood outside and listened through the open windows. When it started raining, they just opened up their umbrellas. On that first Sunday in October the weather was still warm and eight oscillating fans provided some relief from the muggy heat. In a few weeks the weather would turn cold and the only heat in the cement walled church would be the warm bodies crowded together in the pews and in the aisles.

The church service on World Communion Sunday lasted an hour and a half. At the conclusion of the service, many people left. Only those people who had been baptized could stay for the Sacrament of Communion. The pews were still full, but the aisles were now clear and no one was standing outside. Before the communion service could be held, however, there was a service of baptism. One hundred and twenty-five people were baptized in a forty-five minute ceremony. The people being baptized wrote their names on small cards. They kneeled before the altar in groups of about twenty, handed their cards to the pastor so he would know their names completely and accurately, and were sprinkled. I do not know what membership training was required for this commitment.

The communion service began immediately after the baptismal service. Several pastors participated in reading the communion ritual. The congregation sang several hymns including "Break Thou the Bread of Life." Pastor Wang, the senior pastor, then took several trays of a cracker-like material to the altar, and consecrated it. He then broke the crackers into small pieces and the trays were given to eight ushers who distributed them to the worshippers by passing them down each row. On signal by the pastor, everyone then took the "bread" together. The pastor then took trays of small individual glasses of wine to the altar, consecrated it, and this too was distributed to the congregation. The morning services lasted about three hours, and there would be two more services that day at 2:00 and at 7:30.

Nanchang Union Church had three services every Sunday plus several evening services during the week. There were several ministers. Pastor James Wang, the head pastor, was eighty years old. He had been ordained in 1936, had served as a missionary in Korea, had served in Shanghai for a time, and was sent to Nanchang in 1946. Pastor Wang walked bent-over, and he had a slight limp. He looked old until he stepped into the pulpit. Then he had a sparkle in his eyes and preached an hour long sermon with a clear, strong voice. His faith was apparent.

A few weeks before Christmas Pastor Wang asked Leona and me if we wanted to sing in the Christmas service. After our choir experience in Nanjing in 1985 we were hesitant, but Pastor Wang encouraged us and said, "And bring your friends." We said, "We will be happy to."

We still had the Chinese pinyin (Chinese sounds written in Roman letters so we could pronounce them) for "O

Come, All Ye Faithful" from when we had sung in Nanjing. We asked our four American colleagues from Colorado to join us, and we began practicing and learning two verses in Chinese. It would have been difficult to rehearse with the church pianist, so we practiced with a guitar.

On Christmas Sunday, Ron, one of our friends from Colorado, strapped the guitar on his back, and we all climbed on our bicycles, and went to church. It was cold, but fortunately it was not raining. We wore long underwear, down jackets, stocking caps, and gloves. The church was extra full, although compared with the normal over-flowing conditions that seemed impossible. Since we would be singing, we were led through the crowd down to a front pew.

A few minutes after we were seated Pastor Wang greeted each of us warmly, and then to Leona and me quietly said, "We do not consider a guitar as an acceptable instrument for a formal worship service."

We passed the word along, "We will have to sing a capella."

After the opening elements of the service were concluded, a group of 19 women, sitting in the front pews on the other side, stood up, faced the congregation, and in Chinese sang "Hark the Herald Angels Sing." They were all over eighty years old. A man leaned over and told me, "We call them the 'Old Sisters'" Then another group of women, somewhat younger, stood and sang, "Silent Night." After two more groups of women sang, it was our turn. We stood up in a row, looked out at almost a thousand men and women, and began to sing, "O Come All Ye Faithful" in Chinese. At first the congregation, though friendly and expectant, seemed passive. Then as they realized we were singing in Chinese, their faces lighted up, and we could see the broad smiles. Some of them moved their hands and arms, and we could feel the warmth in that cold church. It was a touching scene for them and for us.

The choir presented two beautiful anthems, and a brass quintet played "Brighten the Corner Where You Are," and, of course, there was a sermon an hour long. The large Christmas tree in the corner was a bit bedraggled, but the spirit and enthusiasm of the congregation was exciting. Following the service the choir invited the six of us to sit with them for a picture with their camera.

We then went out into the courtyard and were besieged by well-wishers, all speaking rapidly in Chinese. (Well, hadn't we sung in Chinese?)

As the six of us were riding our bicycles through the heavy Sunday traffic, one of our American colleagues leaned over and said, "I have never seen a group of Chinese more friendly." I responded, "Yes, we've found that Chinese Christians are very responsive."

Esther

Shortly after Easter we were greeting folks in the courtyard after a church service when a young woman spoke to us in English. It was refreshing to be able to talk to someone and get beyond "Hello, how are you?" Her name was Wang Xi Ming. She told us she was a middle school English teacher. She was tall, about five feet six, attractive, and single. After talking for several minutes, she asked if she could visit us, and we set a time for Tuesday afternoon.

On Tuesday we talked for some time about her teaching, and about her brother, and her parents. We served tea and oranges. Wang Xi Ming was bright-eyed and talkative. Since we had met her at church we asked her if she were a Christian. She said that she had been attending church regularly, but that we had not seen her because she normally went to a house church, also called a Preaching Point, near her home. She said that she planned on being baptized soon. She said she had not told her parents that she was attending church. Even though she lived at home, she would leave each Sunday morning without telling them where she was going. She asked if we would attend her baptism. She also asked, "When I am baptized, will you give me a Christian name?"

We felt very humble. We were quite familiar with the Biblical significance of names used to confirm new covenant relationships with God, e. g. Abraham, Paul, and Peter. We told her that we would be very proud to give her a Christian name, but we would have to think and pray about it.

Wang Xi Ming came to our apartment again the following week, and we named her, "Esther." We told her about the *Book of Esther* in the Bible and how the Biblical Esther was described as beautiful, brave and loyal. Esther was very pleased with her Christian name, and she took home one of our Bibles so that she could read *her* book, *Esther.*

About a month later Esther was baptized. The pastor of her house church was not ordained, so the house church worshippers had to go to the Nanchang Union Church for the Sacrament of Baptism. On that Sunday fifty people from her house church were baptized.

While we were waiting for the service of baptism to begin, we witnessed a heated discussion among the pastors. Pastor Wang wanted to baptize by complete immersion, but there was a hole in the baptismal tank. In order to be immersed they would have to delay the baptismal service until the tank could be repaired. The people to be baptized were emotionally ready to be baptized right then and did not want to be put off. There were four pastors involved and they all had something to say. Finally they all left the sanctuary and went to one of the offices to resolve the problem in private. After a ten minute delay, two pastors returned and performed the Sacrament of Baptism by sprinkling. Pastor Wang did not return.

Esther had requested that we take pictures of the baptismal service for her. The persons being baptized went up to the altar in groups of five. It was a touching though simple ceremony. Throughout the entire baptismal service the congregation sang, "O Happy Day, Happy Day, When Jesus Washed My Sins Away," in Chinese. It was a happy day for Esther. Following the ceremony, she had us take pictures of her and her pastor, her and her friends, and someone else took pictures of Esther with us.

Two weeks later Esther and a young pastor took us on an outing to the Pagoda by the river and then to a restaurant to further celebrate the occasion.

Since Esther does not feel she can share her Christian experience with her parents, she has looked to us as her Christian parents. In the closing weeks of our stay in Nanchang Esther visited us several times. We talked, we played tennis, we went for walks, and on Mother's Day Esther gave Leona a Mother's Day card.

Pre-Liberation Methodist Property

Pastor Wang knew that Leona and I were United Methodists so he asked us one day if we would like to see the property the Methodist Church had owned before Liberation in 1949. The Methodist Church owned about 12 to 15 acres of choice property at that time. We were eager to go, so Pastor Wang set a mid-week date for the following week. At the appointed hour we met a young male pastor and a female member of the choir at the church, and we all rode bicycles over to Pastor Wang's home.

We were led into a community courtyard, up a rickety flight of stairs, and into a two room apartment where Pastor Wang, and his elderly wife, greeted us warmly. (His wife was recovering from cataract surgery.) The apartment was austere. Sitting in an uncomfortable wooden chair, I surveyed the room. There were two other chairs and a small table. The floor was made of wooden boards. On one wall there was a picture of The Last Supper and on the opposite wall a picture of the face of Jesus. The only other picture was a calendar. As we sipped a Chinese orange drink, Pastor Wang showed us his meager library, on a shelf in his bedroom, and told how all of his books had been burned during the Cultural Revolution. (We gave him several of our books when we left China.)

From Pastor Wang's porch we could see the old Baldwin School for Girls, a pre-Liberation Methodist School, now the government controlled Number Ten Middle School. Pastor Wang then took us on a walking tour past the old dormitories where the students stayed and past apartment houses where teachers and staff had lived. All of these buildings are still used. We then walked down to the river, and looked at the former Methodist Hospital, now Jiangxi Number One Hospital. We walked past more staff housing until we reached the Number Seven Middle School which formerly was the Methodist Boys School. Pastor Wang told us the principal of the Methodist Boys School was William Johnson, a friend of his occasional neighbor Chiang Kai Shek.

Next to the Boys School, now Number Seven Middle School, and currently under the control of the Middle School, is the former Methodist Church. We could see where the small stained glass windows had been removed, and Pastor Wang told us where the crosses had been. A rock wall had been built across the cement steps leading up from the street, closing off the public entrance. Next door was the house where the Chinese district superintendent had lived over forty years ago and a separate house for the pastor. The building is still being used for living quarters. The church was large. The sanctuary plus balcony would have held over one thousand worshippers. The building is currently being minimally used as a warehouse for a government owned newspaper.

We asked Pastor Wang about the future of the church building. He said that two years ago the government promised to return the church building to the Nanchang Union Church organization, but they had made no progress in carrying out the government promise. Pastor Wang said, "Things in China take time."

Chapter VI

The More Things Change

Pepsi Cola Comes to China

When we were teaching in Nanjing in 1985/86 we occasionally went to the Friendship Store to shop for woven carpets, lacquer ware or other Chinese specialty merchandise. The Friendship Store also carried some western goods. One day we spied a bottle of Pepsi-cola. It was a party size bottle with its tell-tale red, white, and blue Pepsi-cola logo. In spite of all the lovely silk and jade products. the cloisonne and double-faced embroidery, to us Americans who hadn't read a western newspaper in several months, or tasted a hamburger and fries, and had to live on Chinese orange soda, there's something very attractive about a bottle of Pepsi-cola. We asked the clerk the price of that bottle (there was only one). The price was high, and "You must pay in foreign exchange currency." We received fifty percent of our low teachers' salary in tourist money, but that did not go very far. We resisted the temptation.

A couple weeks later we were again in the Friendship Store and as soon as we went in, we went straight for the beverage counter to see if that bottle of Pepsi were still there. It was—at least we assumed it was—the same bottle because now there was a two week's accumulation of dust on it. Each time we entered the Friendship Store we looked for the Pepsi bottle, and after a while we noticed the level of the liquid was about two inches lower. We never did buy that bottle of Pepsi cola.

During the National Day celebration on the Jiangxi Teachers' University campus in 1990 we were feted at a banquet. The beverages that were served were Chinese beer, Sprite, and Pepsi cola. The day after the banquet we took a five hour bus trip through the countryside to a mountain resort area. As we passed through small villages, I could see from the bus window the red, white, and blue Pepsi logo on shelves in small shops along the road.

Pepsi is a symbol to us of the new western products that are now imported, or the western type products that are produced here in China. We can buy Gerber or Heinz baby foods, Kodak film, and American Greeting cards. We can also buy catsup, Kleenex type tissue, napkins and western type toilet paper. We still cannot buy a western newspaper or a hamburger, but we can buy towels with Mickey Mouse or Donald Duck designs.

Pepsi cola has had a greater impact on Chinese life than as just a beverage. We ate in a little Chinese noodle shop one day. When the cook reached for his bottle of cooking oil, he reached for the Pepsi bottle. Most cooking oil is sold in bulk. The clerk pumps it out of a fifty gallon oil drum, but you have to provide your own container. One jin of cooking oil fits nicely into a plastic Pepsi bottle. The bicycle repair shop uses a Pepsi bottle for machine oil. The water supply in China is not drinkable until it is boiled. When people travel by train, they carry their own water—frequently in a Pepsi bottle. We found no Tupperware in China. The Pepsi bottle is a convenient refrigerator container.

Our shower leaks and drips into the bathtub. Because of the shape of the tub, the dripping sounded like a bass drum, until we set a Pepsi bottle under the drip. Now the water splashes along the sloping sides of the bottle and is noiseless. We bought a flower bulb, but what could we use for a pot; we cut off the bottom four inches of a Pepsi bottle. We did not throw away the top of the bottle. We used that for a funnel.

Yesterday we attended a class Christmas party. There was a Christmas tree which had been decorated by the Chinese students. There, hanging from a branch was a lantern ornament made with gold paper fashioned around, you guessed it, a Pepsi bottle.

Mr. Xie

Mr. Xie was one of our Chinese colleagues. He taught Listening six hours a week in the Training Center, and he also taught other courses in the Foreign Languages Department of the main university. We did not know what he included in his Listening Class. We did know that each student was issued a head set, and Mr. Xie played tapes from a console in the teacher's desk.

One day there was a knock at our door. It was Mr. Xie with a folder in one hand and a tape recorder in the other. He had been using a text book with supporting tapes in his Listening Class, but he wanted more authentic exercises, so he had taped several programs from The Voice of America. He then played these programs over and over while he typed out the complete script. We thought this was very creative and commendable, but what did he want us to do? In order to insure accuracy, he wanted us to listen to the tapes and proofread his manuscript.

It was an innovative instructional idea. We were also aware of the tremendous effort, the time that he had obviously spent in listening to the tapes and typing the manuscripts, and his accuracy was impressive. Leona and I found that proofreading was also time consuming and we were native speakers. We had to replay portions of the tapes several times to complete the gaps or correct the few errors Mr. Xie had made. From then on Mr. Xie brought us manuscripts on a weekly basis, and at the end of the year he had produced a complete booklet of programs for general Listening Classroom work.

Mr. Xie was chairperson of the supervisory committee for the Middle School Teachers Program. We met about twice a month and the meetings were held in our apartment. When it turned cold our apartment was about 52 or 53 degrees Fahrenheit. On one of those cold mornings Mr. Xie arrived a few minutes early for the meeting and after the preliminary greetings he asked, "Are you wearing enough clothes?" We promptly pulled up a pant leg and proudly showed off our two layers of long underwear. Then he raised his pant leg and revealed three layers. He then admonished us, "Wear more clothes!" We thought this scene was rather ridiculous; everyone sitting around, pulling their pant legs up, or opening their neck lines to compare their many layers, but it was terribly cold, and this was an experience we all shared. The Chinese felt that Americans did not wear enough layers of clothes. One said, "Americans eat their clothes," meaning they are overweight and then wear fewer clothes. Leona and I did lose forty-five pounds combined in our first year in China.

One day in mid-May, 1991, I was sitting on the steps of the Administration Building on the Jiangxi Teachers University campus and Mr. Xie walked by. It was about 9:00 in the morning.

"Where are you going?"

Mr. Xie said, "Today is Children's Day. There is no school today, and I am going to take my son to the park."

Mr. Xie, like many fathers, and mothers too, did not have the opportunity to spend much time with their children. Men and women worked six days a week, and on their day off, they were very busy shopping, doing laundry and housework and other chores. During the week the children went to school until 4:30 p.m., then played with their friends until supper time, and then had homework most evenings. Although teachers had the summers off, factory and office workers never had any vacations at all. They only took time off for the occasional holiday. Mr. Xie was anticipating a day with his eleven year old son. The son had wanted to go to the park earlier, but Mr. Xie had something he had to do first. Now, he was on his way home, to his apartment just off campus.

I talked with Mr. Xie the following day.

"Well, how was your day in the park with your son?"

Mr. Xie responded, "I did not go."

I asked, "What happened?"

He said, "My son was hanging around the house, waiting for me to come home. He became restless and bored. Then some of his friends came by and said, 'Let's go to the park.' My wife said, 'No.' Xiao Xie said, 'Can I go, can I go, please!' Finally my wife had to give in."

I could see the hurt in Mr. Xie's eyes. His son had preferred to go to the park with his friends rather than wait for his father, and that was his only son.

Toward the end of the school year in 1991 Mr. Xie invited Leona and me to his home for supper. It was a simple supper, served informally, and without fanfare. Leona and I felt like we were colleagues and friends, rather than foreign guests. Mrs. Xie served several dishes, and then sat down briefly and ate with us, but since she did not speak English, she did not linger at the table afterwards. Mr. Xie's son did not eat with us. He came to the table late, picked out the food that he wanted, put it on a plate, and then carried it into the other room so he could watch television.

After dinner Mr. Xie began reminiscing about his past. He told us that he was born in a small village in the southern part of Jiangxi Province. He said that several hundred years ago a family settled in that remote area, and with subsequent generations, a village has developed, but everyone is related. Today the village is 15 kilometers from the nearest town and there is no road.

Mr. Xie said he lived in the village until he was middle school aged, then each Monday morning he walked 15 kilometers to school, stayed in a dormitory through the week, and then on Saturday afternoons he would walk home.

The village still does not have electricity, and does not have or use anything that cannot be carried in on someone's back. The people raise their own food which consists of rice, pork, fish, chicken and ducks, vegetables, and fruit. We asked if they had sugar. He said they use honey primarily. We asked if they used lights. He said they do carry in some kerosene for lamps, but use them sparingly. He also said that no one has to lock their doors. He told one story to exemplify the honesty of the village: a man had an apple tree, but he did not pick the apples. The apples started falling on the ground. Two boys came by and picked up some of the apples that had fallen on the ground and took them home. When their father saw them with the apples, he marched them back to the owner of the apple tree, and made the boys return the apples. The owner then realized his apples were going to waste, so he picked them all and gave them to his neighbors.

Mr. Xie said he was the only one from the village that had ever gone to a university. We did not know the circumstances, but we do know that he had studied in Shanghai and one of his favorite professors was a woman from Britain. He learned English and teaching methodology well.

Mr. Xie had last seen his father five years before. He added, "It is a difficult trip." He said his son had never seen his grandfather. In between visits, however, Mr. Xie had written to his father, and sometimes in response to specific needs, had sent his father money. His most recent money order had been for fertilizer. (Mr. Xie never mentioned his mother.)

Seventy-eight percent of the people in China live in the country-side. Because it is a large country, the country-side experience varies widely, and because there is limited mobility among the population, villages and towns remain isolated socially as well as physically.

How is China Changing[1]

As I ate my morning bowl of watery rice gruel at the Jiangxi Teachers University, I reflected on the fact that rice has served as the basic diet for millions of people for five thousand years. I had watched women in the countryside still harvesting rice with their hand scythes, and men with their carry-poles carrying rice bundles to the threshing floors. The age-less water buffalo were pulling plows through harvested fields to continue the timeless cycle. Eighty percent of the population live in the countryside. I lived and taught English in a little-developed city where one million Chinese live in post Liberation (1949) brick apartment houses. I say *Chinese* because by American standards their population is very homogeneous. In the 1990 census the Han nationality made up ninety-two percent of the population.

In the cities the streets are filled with hundreds of bicycles weaving in and around the pull carts that are buried under unbelievable loads. The two-wheeled carts have served as a basic vehicle for drayage for thousands of years, and to look at them, one wonders if some of them are not the original carts.

Across the street from the university gate there is an open market, an alley really, with stalls lining both sides. I had purchased oranges, bananas, apples and pears along the right side, a half jin at a time, and generally avoided the slabs of pork resting on tables and benches exposed to the elements on the left. Farther down the alley were dried persimmons, walnuts in season, breads and cookies, and then the plastic utensils, china-ware seconds, bolts of cloth, and knitting yarn. These were the free market vendors whose numbers have exploded with the loosening of the economy in China.

A retired Chinese professor told me that eight years ago, there were no free market stalls in this city. Now when I

---

[1] An unpublished article written in Nanchang, China, in 1991.

ride a bicycle down town, I see goods displayed on the side walk in the underpass, small frogs in net bags, sweaters and rain coats, leather jackets. I saw a man, one day, holding a dead pheasant, haggling over the price, with four more laying at his feet. In the main square special sales days bring hundreds of vendors, displaying their wares on single width beds that unfold and provide six foot sales counters. The merchandise includes clothing, hardware, food, and appliances. Vegetables are sold on street corners, along the sidewalk, and in alley stalls as well as in semi-enclosed "farmers markets" that include eggs, fish, poultry, and meat.

The October 4, 1990 *China Daily* described this new free market enterprise as follows:

> Faced with a protracted shortage of non-staple food supplied to its urban consumers, China initiated a bold reform of the vegetable and food market across the country in the mid-1980's, giving free rein to private operations of food marketing. The reform proved highly successful, as Chinese city dwellers now get almost seventy per cent of their daily non-staple food from the free market.

Other free market services are also available. Just outside the university gate there are four shoe repairmen, sitting on four legged stools about six inches high, with their assortment of old tires for rubber, extra heels, metal heel clips, and pedal sewing machines. Mixed in with the shoe repairmen are two vendors anxious to make duplicate keys. Fifty feet beyond is a bicycle repairman with his tools in the back of a pedal driven cargo tricycle. Prospective customers do not have to cross the street; there is an equal number of services available there as well. When the weather is warm one may find tailors seated at portable sewing machines on the sidewalk, and when the weather turns cold, vendors bake sweet potatoes in barrels. Barbers set up their barber chairs out on the sidewalk as well.

I have seen a greater variety of western and western-type goods this year. When my wife and I taught in Nanjing in 1985/86, we looked in dozens of different stores over a period of two weeks before we found western type toilet paper in the student store at a neighboring university. Now two different Chinese brands of western type toilet paper is available in all of the local department stores. Tissue resembling kleenex, small luncheon napkins, and sanitary napkins are also available. One can buy Sprite, catsup, millet crisp crust (corn chips), something called margara resembling butter, orange juice, and yogurt—a bottled drink.

Chinese seem to have more money and are buying more things. Five years ago a few Chinese were getting refrigerators, black and white televisions, and a simple model washing machine in which the agitator remained fixed and the basket rotated. Today refrigerators and televisions are much more plentiful. We are using a washing machine that not only agitates, but has a spin dryer as well. Hair dryers, portable ovens, and video cassette recorders are in the stores and being purchased by some.

We have seen a greater variety of clothing on display and a greater concern for fashion. On a tour in nineteen eighty we saw drab green and blue pants and jackets, and most of the shirts and blouses were made from white cloth. Five years later we were impressed with the variety of color we saw in clothing in general, and we noticed many co-eds were wearing dresses rather than pants. Today we see not only a greater variety of clothing on display, but there are also fashion specialty shops. The young women we work with show much greater concern for stylish appearance.

We went to the city park to enjoy the beautiful chrysanthemum displays that were arranged in shapes of peacocks and dragons and other animals. It was a warm day, and we were chatting with a group of school children on their outing to the park when a disheveled, ragged and dirty peasant walked up to us. He was carrying a small child, perhaps three years old, and at first I did not know what he wanted. Then he showed me several small bills in his hand and asked me for money. We were surprised. In Nanjing five years ago we seldom saw a person who looked this destitute, and were never asked for money. Since then we have been approached almost on a weekly basis when coming out of the Sunday church service by a man carrying a child, or by a person dragging a crooked leg, or by a peasant woman inside the church itself. We are under the impression that begging is illegal in China and the authorities are trying to discourage it, but several from the church congregation did give them money.

Our students this year are a special class of middle-aged middle school teachers who have returned to college for one year of re-training. Our class monitor, Deng Xi Jen, who has been teaching for twenty years, received a telephone call requesting his immediate presence at his home in Shang Rao County. Apparently his house had been burglarized last April. He had lost five thousand yuan in cash and bank credit slips, and the police had just uncovered some clues regarding the incident. Since then one of our women students has had twenty-two yuan stolen from her purse while she was shopping in a downtown department store, and another student lost a down comforter off her bed in one of the dormitories. These incidents are from a class of only twenty-four students. There was very little crime in China five years ago. We did not have to watch our wallets until we went to Hong Kong. Now we are told to be very careful everywhere.

Although many changes are taking place in China, the Western observer should not assume that a Western style democracy is right around the corner. Today you cannot buy a Western magazine or newspaper in this city of one million. In the reference library of the Foreign Language Department of this university there are place cards for *Time*, *Readers Digest*, and *The National Geographic*, but there are no magazines. In response to my inquiry they said, "Maybe next year." The western tourist is impressed with CNN news on television in the tourist hotels in Shanghai and

Beijing, but we have not found any newscasts in English in this city. Furthermore, there is a large satellite disc on this campus which the authorities asked to be disconnected because it allowed too much access to western television.

I am living in a conservative city in southern China, but in every city people must take their packages to the post office unwrapped so they may be inspected before they are mailed, and my family informs me that four out of five of our letters sent to the United States have been slit.

China's recognition of religious freedom has been included as part of their modernization. In the December 6, 1990 issue of the *China Daily* it stated that Li Peng, premier of China, "stressed in Beijing yesterday the importance of handling religious affairs well and implementing correctly the policy of protecting the freedom of religious belief." In the December 10 issue, however, the *China Daily* stated, "Many religious affairs officials complained that local leaders placed little importance in and understood little about religious affairs." The director of China's Religious Affairs Bureau, Ren Wuzhi, said, "Communist Party members and officials of various levels would be instructed in religious policy *in the next few years*" (italics added).

Meanwhile the Amity Foundation, a non-governmental social services organization, in joint-venture with the United Bible Societies developed a printing plant in 1987 just outside Nanjing for the primary purpose of printing Bibles. By August 1990 the plant had printed two million Bibles and the goal for 1991 is another 1.6 million. According to the December 10, *China Daily* China has a religious population of about one hundred million, including seventeen million Muslims, three million Catholics and four million Protestants. The largest religious group is Buddhist.

There have been many changes in China attributable to the June fourth (1989) student protests. The world is aware of the immediate drop in tourism and in international trade and in new business ventures. Foreign investments began to recover in April 1990, and tourism has now returned to near 1989 levels as well.

China continues to send large numbers of scholars to western universities, but now requires five years teaching or work experience first. China hopes the older students will have more reason to return after the study has been completed. Living conditions for Chinese students and teachers have improved regarding more heat, some air conditioning, carpeting, refrigerators, and washing machines, but more restrictions on foreign teachers' contact with Chinese students. At this university we live in a guest house compound with a gate attendant. Students must register at the entrance before visiting us. We may not have more than four students at any one time, and all students must leave by ten o'clock p. m. We are told that this procedure is *for our protection.*

In the November 7, 1990 issue of the *China Daily* an article appeared with the following headline, "Rules to ensure college order." The article included the following:

> "...the drafting of the regulations and efforts to improve management had nothing to do with the student unrest last year," but added that "if a better job was made of college management, campus order and stability would be improved."
>
> "Public lectures and speeches that run against the basic rules of China's constitution and education policy, or that spread superstition and deal with religious activities, are banned, as are unauthorized organizations, illegal publications and broadcasting on campus, according to the new regulations."
>
> "...journalists from home and abroad must get permits before interviewing and reporting on activities within the campus."

Chinese students are discouraged from getting too close to foreign teachers, and to help prevent that, foreign teachers are limited to two consecutive years at any one college.

So China is changing and during any period of change, one may find elements of the old: a month ago in front of the department store where we shop a peasant was standing with two tiny baby girls wrapped in blankets laying on the ground; he was trying to sell them, and elements of the new: in a grove of large bamboo just outside the city there is graffiti scratched into the bamboo supporting free speech, democracy, and the June Fourth student movement (June 4, 1989, in Tiananmen Square.)

Yes, China is changing, but a country so large, and with so many people, the change will come very slowly.

Chapter VII

Welcome Home

We were scheduled to leave Beijing on Thursday morning, July 26, at eight thirty. We were required to check in at the airport at six-thirty. We were staying at the Guest House of the National Defense Department, (this was possible because we knew someone), and it was about forty-five minutes from the airport. That meant we would have to leave by five-forty-five a. m.

Our friend had arranged a car on several occasions, but this time we needed a station wagon because of all of our luggage. Our friend would ask the driver to bring the station wagon the night before, stay over night in the guest house and be ready to take us at the early hour. When she checked with the driver he declined, saying his license plate was an odd number, and he was not authorized to drive on even numbered days. Our friend then asked her brother, who had even numbered license plates, but he could not come the evening before because that would be arriving on an odd numbered day. (As I understand it, this only applies to station wagons.)

On Thursday morning, at five-forty-five a. m., we left for the Beijing airport. We passed through customs without opening a bag, and by seven o'clock we were in the lobby, waiting. One minor problem—I still had almost five hundred yuan in my pocket, and it is illegal to take Chinese money out of the country. I had not worried about this because people had assured me there was a bank at the airport. What they didn't tell me was, it won't be open at seven o'clock in the morning.

At that point I found out we had to pay an airport tax, forty yuan each. No problem. I still had about four hundred yuan. I asked an employee what time the bank opened. He thought about eight o'clock a. m. Our plane would take off at eight-thirty. We would still have to go through the security check, and then allow time for boarding. Of course, the lobby was filled with merchandise sales counters. So, we bought something, a beautiful cloisonne vase. I don't know whether it was what we really wanted, or whether it was because it cost the right amount—almost four hundred yuan. I felt good about our purchase though; they weren't going to cause us to lose our money—and then the bank opened. It was seven-forty a. m. "Oh, well!"

I still had some small change. The post office also opened, so I spent every last cent on a variety of stamps for my grandchildren.

The United Airlines plane took off on schedule. In two hours we would stop briefly in Shanghai and then a couple more hours to Tokyo. We would be back in the United States the same morning. I felt good about the morning. Everything had gone according to schedule. We had had minimal problems handling our four large suitcases. We got rid of our Chinese money, and we had notified our family of the expected arrival time in San Francisco.

It had been a long and eventful year. I remembered that first day the middle school teachers arrived; they were so scared. They wanted to do well with their new foreign teachers, but most of them could not understand our English. Then in October when Leona got sick and had to go to the hospital; we were so scared because we couldn't understand the doctors' Chinese. I remembered the fun times we had had in class, especially the informal Monday evening sessions. Our students entered into the games and laughed at each other's antics. They also enjoyed the singing. The Christmas season: the class party, singing at church, all the cards and greetings. And we really enjoyed New Year's at Nancy and Bob's, and the dancing on New Year's Eve.

The closing events were memorable, everyone saying good bye. The Training Center had given us autograph books and all the students had to sign them. "I will be your friend *forever!*" "You will always be my teacher!" And just as we arrived at the restaurant for the final party, Kent lit all those firecrackers. And how un-elegant it seemed to raise a rice bowl of warm beer and present a toast, but how moving it was to see all those happy faces as they did it. I wondered if I would feel excited when we actually left China's air space; that would be just a few more hours.

The flight to Shanghai was uneventful. All passengers got off the plane, entered the terminal, and then went through a passport check. At twelve o'clock we got back on the plane, and by twelve-fifteen were taxiing down the runway. We would be in Tokyo by two-thirty. The plane tried to make a turn to head into the wind, but it would not turn. The hydraulic system failed. We were towed back to the terminal building. All of the passengers got off the plane and went back into the terminal again. There was no place to sit down so we walked around. There were lots of sales counters, but now we had no Chinese money. I had so efficiently disposed of that in Beijing. We waited. It was hot and muggy. At five o'clock we were told we would take off in fifteen minutes. At five-fifteen we were told the hydraulic system had not passed the service test and we would have to spend the night in Shanghai. We could phone our family in California and say we would not arrive the next morning, but we could not yet tell them when we would arrive. Fortunately, one thing our China experience had taught us was patience.

We were taken to the Hilton Hotel, luxurious and beautiful. From our nineteenth floor window we looked out across the city of Shanghai. We laid on our king size bed and watched CNN on color television. We enjoyed a salad bar and buffet, (our first salad bar in one year), in the Garden Room while we listened to classical music played by a stringed quartet. Everything was paid for by United Airlines. We returned to our room and I looked for the thermos of boiled water. There wasn't any thermos, anywhere. "Leona, this isn't China!"

Many people, whether missionaries, peace corps workers, or English teachers, have difficulty re-adjusting to their home country when they return. It had been a long year in America also. Our grandchildren had gone "trick or treating," and celebrated Christmas and Easter and had birthday parties. California elected a new governor in November and suffered a killing freeze in December. The biggest event of all began on January 18. We missed the entire Gulf War. We would have to catch up on many of the events that had occurred at home. Would anyone want to catch up on our events?

We landed in San Francisco. All airports are busy, but in San Francisco everyone speaks English, and the signs are all in English. Customs was routine and making a phone call to our daughter in Palo Alto was simple, just put in a quarter.

After re-uniting with the grandchildren, looking at their latest "treasures" and presenting them with Chinese stamp albums, we toured their house—they had moved to California while we were in China. There was a large kitchen with hot and cold running water, garbage disposal, gas stove **with oven**, large refrigerator, dish washer, micro-wave, mixer, toaster, waffle iron, and walls of cupboards. In the rest of the house we were struck by all the carpeting, and the spaciousness, the drapes on the windows, and the pictures on the walls.

In the bathroom there was a flush toilet, a bathtub, a high quality tile job, and we could use the water right out of the tap to brush our teeth.

"For your first meal back in the United States, what do you want to eat?"

We said, "Tossed green salad with fresh tomatoes, fresh fruit, potato salad, a hamburger, iced tea with lots of ice, and ice cream for dessert."

The next morning we went to the farmers market in Palo Alto. I still did not feel at home. I lacked any sense of belonging. I felt detached from what was happening around me.

The weather was refreshing—sunny and cool, and most important, the air was dry—there was not the muggy feeling of south China. The fruit was amazing. Large ripe peaches, huge red strawberries, apples, plums, tomatoes, dried fruit, melons, corn. This was California. I was also impressed with the size of the people. The men seemed to tower over me, and yet I felt tall when I was in China. The women were also tall and much heavier than the petite Chinese women. Walking among the people that day in farmer's market, I had to consciously avoid touching anyone. There are so many people in China that one constantly bumps into other people or are bumped by them in shops or stores or when just walking down the sidewalk. Body contact is so common, no one turns around to say, "sorry." One soon feels like a pin ball. If two people are standing eight inches apart, someone else will push between you to get to the other side. Americans have a personal space requirement that is not universal. I was conscious of everything around me, but I still felt like a spectator. I was observing America, rather than participating in it.

In a few days we returned to the small valley town where we had our home, but our house was still occupied since it had been rented during our stay in China. We went to the post office and arranged for a post office box. The clerk asked, "Where do you live?" and we did not know what to say. We drove around, looking at all of the new construction, the new post office, a new school, the new Boys and Girls Club, an entire shopping center, and five-hundred new homes, but we were still just observing.

We then traveled to San Diego to visit our younger son and his family. My wife went shopping for a birthday present. She found an inexpensive blouse. She was shocked at the price, however—$20. She thought to herself, "That's almost 100 yuan!" The prices on everything were outrageous. In China I got my hair cut for ten cents, rubber boots for two dollars, and I paid less than six dollars for a windbreaker.

That evening our son took us to an outdoor concert by the San Diego Harbor. The San Diego Symphony played a pops concert of the Big Band era. The first number was the Star Spangled Banner. A spot light displayed the American flag blowing briskly in the ocean breeze. The flag had a special meaning for us now.

There was a small dance platform where my wife and I danced to Tommy Dorsey, Glen Miller, Woody Herman, and Harry James. The music brought back memories of our dating days. As the band was playing the final number there was a fireworks display over the bay. We watched the sky rockets and their showers of red, green, and gold sparkles falling into the bay. It gave me a tingling feeling. We had missed celebrating the Fourth of July the month before. I told my wife, "I think we're home!"